GOLF

Alistair Cooke with Jack Nicklaus at a reception on the eve
of the British Open Championship at St Andrews, 1978

GOLF
THE MARVELOUS MANIA

ALISTAIR
COOKE

FOREWORD BY JACK NICKLAUS
AFTERWORD BY JERRY TARDE

ARCADE PUBLISHING ♀ NEW YORK

FIRST U.S. EDITION 2008

First published in the U.K. as *The Marvellous Mania* by Allen Lane

Frontispiece courtesy the Estate of Alistair Cooke, from the Alistair Cooke
Collection at the Howard Gotlieb Archival Research Center, Boston University

Library of Congress Cataloging-in-Publication Data

Cooke, Alistair, 1908–2004.
  Golf : the marvelous mania / Alistair Cooke ; foreword by Jack Nicklaus ;
afterword by Jerry Tarde. —1st U.S. ed.
      p. cm.
  Includes index.
  ISBN 978-1-55970-873-9 (alk. paper)
  1. Golf—Anecdotes. 2. Golf stories. I. Title.

  GV967.C598 2007
  796.352—dc22   2008006945

Published in the United States by Arcade Publishing, Inc., New York
Distributed by Hachette Book Group USA

Visit our Web site at www.arcadepub.com

10 9 8 7 6 5 4 3 2 1

Designed by Rowland Phototypesetting Ltd.

EB

PRINTED IN THE UNITED STATES OF AMERICA

Contents

Foreword

by Jack Nicklaus

He was known to the British as the presenter of *Letter from America*, the longest-running series in radio history presented by one man. He was known to the Americans as the quintessential Brit, who presented *Masterpiece Theater*, as well as being a highly respected film and jazz critic, and a man whose acclaimed television series *America* won two Emmy Awards. He was known to most of the world as a journalist, but not any ordinary correspondent. This English-born journalist was asked to address the United States Congress on the occasion of its two hundreth anniversary. To my wife Barbara and me, most of all, he was a friend.

Alistair Cooke was many things to many people because he was a man of depth, who was at ease with the great, be they statesmen, politicians, entertainers or sportsmen. Whatever the subject, Alistair's broadcasting and writing were scrupulously honest. His readers and listeners trusted him implicitly. They were also given fresh insight, for Cooke's was an analytical mind trained at Cambridge, Harvard and Yale. Yet everything was presented in a fresh, lyrical manner, with enormous style. These were the gifts he brought to writing about one of the enduring loves of his life, the game of golf.

Athletes are often wary of journalists, particularly those of today's generation, but with Alistair you knew that what he wrote about you was true and displayed uncanny understanding. He did not write to be sensational; he wrote to tell it as it really was. Just as he held up a mirror for the American people to see themselves unadorned in his political commentaries and to come to their own conclusions about events, so it was with his sports writing – and his golf writing in particular. Alistair gave the reader an extraordinary insight into what actually happened. It was almost as if he were not just reporting on the events, but taking part in them too. Some of these tournaments I was fortunate to play in, and one of the joys of reading these articles again has been to relive those moments through his wonderful prose. It is as if they happened only yesterday!

Perhaps one of the great joys to be found in Alistair's writings is his deep respect for one of my childhood heroes, Bob Jones – the heralded amateur golfer after whom I patterned my early career. Cooke met a huge number of famous people, yet he was able to write sincerely of Jones that he was 'one of the three or four finest human beings I have ever known'. No further proof is needed that Alistair, the 'elegant interpreter of America,' was always spot on in his judgement.

I hope you will find in this collection, as I have, something to treasure!

Editor's Note

Golf was a passion Alistair Cooke acquired in late middle age, at 55, but he made up for lost time by playing it well into his nineties and writing about it with the zeal of a convert. If his outpourings about his favourite sport had any overarching purpose, it was, as he put it 'to deter some other intending addict'. *The Marvellous Mania* was the title Alistair gave to his television history of golf, which was never broadcast (for the full story see Nick Clarke's superb biography (Arcade Publishing, 2000, pp. 385–9). The phrase evokes the combined frustrations, delights and challenges of the great game, and is an appropriate title for this collection too. *Fun and Games with Alistair Cooke* (1995) included some of Alistair's golf writings, together with pieces on other sports and entertainments. In bringing all of his golf pieces together for this collection I have added previously uncollected essays and golfing 'Letters from America' with the aim of producing the essential 'Cooke on Golf'. The publisher has added occasional footnotes to elucidate some golfing names and terms that might prove arcane for the modern reader/golfer.

For their help in preparing this book for press I would like to thank: Susan Cooke-Kittredge and the Estate of Alistair Cooke for their support and enthusiasm; Patti Yasek for her tireless energy and commitment to ensuring that the manuscript was kept on track and correctly presented; Stuart Proffitt and Phillip Birch at Penguin, both expert putters; Alex Rankin and Jennifer Richardson at the Alistair Cooke Collection, Howard Gotlieb Archival Research Center at Boston University, for providing some of the lost essays; Jerry Tarde, the editor in chief of *Golf Digest* for permission to include his recollections of AC, and Tara Fucale of *Golf Digest* for her help in tracing other pieces; Martin Davis at The American Golfer, Inc.; Frank D. 'Sandy' Tatum Jr; Tim Jollands and Val Rice for copyediting; and Michael Parkinson for introducing me to Alistair Cooke back in 1975.

In his note to the reader in *Fun and Games*, Alistair wrote of his golfing essays: 'They were written far apart in time but always in grateful relief from the daily grind of a foreign correspondent, who lives in the jungle of politics and who, during this whole period, worked in the menacing chill of the Cold War. For more than fifty years, I can truly say that scarcely a day has gone by when I didn't think about government, its plethora of ailments and its depressing range of failed panaceas. In politics, nothing is ever settle for keeps, nobody wins. In games, the problems are solved: somebody wins. Hence the "isle of joy" offered by a sport in an ocean of anxieties. Down the years, I have found no haven more therapeutic than an absorption first with fishing and, in later years, with playing golf and watching tennis. I have come to feel a deep, unspoken pity for people who have no attachment to a single sport, almost as sorry for them as I am for teetotallers.'

Colin Webb, 2008

GOLF

I

History of the Scottish Torture

1973

They have been playing golf for eight hundred years and nobody has satisfactorily said why.

For of all forms of exercise theoretically designed for recreation and relaxation none can be so unerringly guaranteed to produce nervous exhaustion and despair leading to severe mental illness and, in some cases, petulance. The consolation once offered by a helpful caddie to a British prime minister that it was 'only a game' was enough to unloose a torrent of obscenity that had never before passed the statesman's lips. After an abominable round, a man is known to have slit his wrists with a razor blade and, having bandaged them, to stumble into the locker room and enquire of his partner: 'What time tomorrow?' Bing Crosby had a friend who has been working on his game for forty years and who, when asked after a long absence if he was playing much golf, moodily replied, 'Just days.'

Why should anyone persist in a game whose aim, in Winston Churchill's memorable definition, 'is to hit a small ball into an even smaller hole with weapons singularly ill-designed for the purpose'? Well, it has been going on for so long that it is impossible to dismiss, like mah-jong or sex, as a passing fad. Bernard Shaw once proclaimed that the propulsion of a ball across open country with a stick was 'a typical capitalist lunacy of upper-class Edwardian England'. As usual, he summarily dismissed all the facts in the interests of a sentence with a lilt, for the lunatics so afflicted have remained a hardy race since Roman times at the latest. Caesar's legions instructed the barbarian

Britons in banging a leather ball stuffed with chicken feathers. That ball remained standard until 1845, when an English clergyman who dabbled in Hindu mythology received a statue from India of the god Vishnu wrapped in gutta-percha. The cult of Vishnu – incorporating as we all know the notion of 'uncountable incarnations' with the tenth still missing! – is extremely taxing to a mind brought up on the simplicities of the New Testament. And it may well be that the Rev. Dr Robert Adams Patterson saw in the gutta-percha wrapping a saving expression of the grace of God. At any rate, he made out of it the first gutta-percha golf ball and so became immortal. (The opposing school of thought, which maintains that the packaged god was not Vishnu but Siva – The Destroyer – is entitled to its opinion. That's as far as we're going to go just now with the effect of Hinduism on the composition of golf balls.)

Anyway, at some unrecorded point during the 2,000-year dominance of 'the feather' (55 BC–AD 1845) the Dutch banged a ball across a frozen pond at an adjoining post. Since the game itself was called Het Kolven, all the Scotsmen since Robert the Bruce cannot howl down the evidence that golf, in its essentials and its terminology, was a Dutch invention. The Dutch pretty soon saw where it was leading (to paranoia and the paralysis of their empire) and more or less abandoned it. By then the Scots had seized on it and, no later than the fifteenth century, it posed a similar threat to the national defence, causing ordinary citizens who should have been off at archery practice to spend all their spare time trying to hit the damn thing straight. James II of Scotland was sufficiently alarmed at the neglect of archery to put out, in 1457, a decree commanding that 'golfe be utterly cryed down and not to be used'. It was too late. James did not recognise what every other Scot knew in his bones: that golf was just what the Scottish character had been searching for, for centuries. Namely, a method of self-torture, disguised as a game, which would entrap irreligious youths into the principles of what was to become known first as Calvinism and then, through het kolvenism, as 'golf'. The main tenets of this faith are that life is grim and uncomfortable and that human vanity cannot prevail. The emblem on the necktie reserved for the members of the Royal and Ancient Golf Club of St Andrews – the Vatican of golf – is of St Andrew himself bearing the saltire cross on which, once he was captured at Patras, he was to be stretched before he was crucified. Only the Scots would have thought of celebrating a national game with the figure of a tortured saint. Yet, as anyone knows who has laboured for years to put together a serviceable golf game and seen it collapse in a single afternoon, the symbol is apt. No experienced golfer has ever suggested that St Andrew is a morbid choice as the patron saint of the game. He was a realist moving towards a sticky end, and he triumphantly exemplified the golfer's credo: that Man should expect very little here below and strive to get it. If there is one generalisation that may be applied to the inveterate golfer, it is that he is never an idealist. It is impossible to imagine Ibsen, Dante, Shaw, Hitler or D. H. Lawrence sallying out on a Saturday afternoon to subject his ego so publicly to the facts of life. Of all European nations, the Germans are the non-golfing champions. The game is too much for their pride. For every game of golf is an open exhibition of overweening ambition, courage deflated by stupidity, skill soured by a whiff of arrogance. It is possible to fake a reasonable bridge game and to affect a modestly consistent skill at swimming, billiards and, yes, tennis. Even a mediocre chess player can convey, with a little adroit gamesmanship, that he was plotting a combination that didn't quite come off. But every golfer, no matter how impressively he has talked up, or talked down, his game beforehand, proclaims in the simple act of standing to the ball – before he has even started to swing – that he is a 10 handicap or an incurable 25. It does not take a pro to recognise, after a hole or two, that A is a fake and B is a duffer and C – goddammit! – is a golfer. (There are baffling exceptions. It is quite clear from watching the swing of Doug Sanders* and

* Doug Sanders (b. 1933): American golfer, turned pro in 1957 and won twenty PGA tournaments.

the stunted finish of Arnold Palmer that neither of them will ever be a golfer.)

These humiliations are the essence of the game. They derive from the fact that the human anatomy is exquisitely designed to do practically anything but play golf. To get an elementary grasp of the game, a human must learn, by endless practice, a continuous and subtle series of highly unnatural movements, involving about sixty-four muscles, that result in a seemingly 'natural' swing, taking all of two seconds to begin and end. Very few of us ever make it, and then not for long. No one makes it for ever. Jack Nicklaus, the best golfer of our day, and perhaps of any day, is at this moment busy working on some puzzling 'defect' in his swing.

Yet the figures on the national addiction to golf are almost as alarming as the hard-drug statistics. When tennis was born, a century ago, the Scots had been at golf for five hundred years at least. But there were no known American golfers. (It was tried out in New York, South Carolina and Georgia at the end of the eighteenth century and given up as hopeless.) Twenty years ago, there were calculated to be eight million hooked Americans; today, it is closer to fourteen million.

There must be good reasons. The usual ones given by golfers to non-golfers are three:

1. That the game, unlike tennis, squash, pinochle, chess, *boccie** and practically every other competitive joust, is not played on the same dull rectangle or board or in the identical pit or alley the world over but is played across delightful varieties of open landscape. I should like very much to maintain that all golfers are nature lovers. Unfortunately, while all golfers know the difference between a bunker and a hole in the ground, legions of them cannot tell a cypress from a Cypriot.

2. That there is something tonic and bracing about the fact that you are totally responsible for the fate of the little white ball and that

---

* *boccie*: Italian game similar to bowls, but played with wooden balls on a long, narrow gravel-covered court.

you have only one chance of hitting it correctly (there is no second serve, no third strike, no fourth down, etc.).

3. That golf offers the supreme challenge of playing, not against an opponent, but always and only against yourself.

The second and third reasons simply detail the objections, not the incentives, to playing golf and powerfully confirm what I seem to have been saying all along, that no man in his right mind would ever play golf. That is just the point. Nobody in his right mind does, no mature adult with a grain of what the French call *l'amour-propre*, which has nothing to do with girls and everything to do with self-respect. Right-minded men fish, grow petunias, run the PTA or the White House. (The best thing about Eisenhower's presidency was his Jeffersonian conviction that there should be as little government and as much golf as possible.)

So right at the start you can be sure, wherever you wander to pick up a game, that there are certain noxious types you will never have to meet. The proud, the self-regarding, the anxious. Anybody concerned for his 'image' gave up golf as soon as he saw that his partners, in a single round, had fathomed his deep pretentiousness. Look at the membership board of any fashionable club and you will see fashionable names, all right. But you will also notice that there is no handicap number against their names. They are non-playing members, for the simple reason that they have no intention of exhibiting, week in and week out, what their friends know anyway, that they are pompous asses. Show me a man in a round of golf and I will give you a character analysis that makes Jeane Dixon* look like – well, Jeane Dixon.

The main reason, I believe, for the lure of golf has to do with a unique brand of companionship possible only to a psychological type that unites the little boy aching to be king with the sensible adult who knows he'll never make it. It is the companionship of

---

* Jeane Dixon (1918–1997): American astrologer who prophesied Kennedy's assassination. She also, controversially, advised Nancy Reagan.

communal, low-key debunking, a willingness to invest three or four hours in proving to one and all the vanity of human wishes – especially the vanity of your closest friends. 'When a man laughs at his troubles,' Mencken wrote, 'he loses a good many friends; they never forgive the loss of the prerogative.' Mencken* abominated golfers and did not know them. If he had, he would have discovered the only world-wide secret society that revels in the mutual display of human frailty. By providing every man with the visible proof that his partner is a failing show-off, golf reinforces one of the great joys of friendship; it is all the more delicious for being secret, since the etiquette of golf requires that you keep it to yourself.

Don't suppose, though, that golfers are a particular species of meanie. They are a special kind of moral realist who nips the normal romantic and idealistic yearnings in the bud by proving once or twice a week that life is unconquerable but endurable. For the golfer compresses into a few hours all the emotions he spreads over the rest of his life: hope, envy, betrayal, self-discipline, self-deceit, the Holy Grail in view, the Grail smartly whipped out of sight. You're away, partner.

---

* H. L. Mencken (1880–1956): American journalist, political commentator and literary critic.

2

Fun and Games at Blackpool

1972

I don't know when I first became aware that my mother's morning battle with her bronchia was abnormal: that people do not usually bark away like a pack of wolves on getting up in the morning. It was a frightening sound to strangers but, being a small boy and therefore accepting almost everything about our family life as normal, I took it for granted, just as I took for granted the endless dark mornings, the blanket of smog, the slippery veil of mud on the streets, which only later did I discover were not typical of life on this globe but only of life in Manchester.

'It was her cough that carried her off,' my mother's friends would chant, with the peculiar cheerful grimness of Lancashire people. Happily, it took quite some time. She bore it for eighty-six years. But it was her cough that first took us from Salford to Blackpool. Towards the end of 1916, after a particularly harrowing bout, the doctor told us that the Manchester climate was not meant for her (the implication that it was meant for anybody is another interesting facet of Lancashire phlegm; and phlegm, I think, is the right word). He solemnly announced that she should move to either of two places: to Blackpool or Egypt! Since my father, a Methodist lay preacher and an artist in metal work (who fashioned the flagship that serves as a weathervane atop the Town Hall), had gone into an aeroplane factory by way of doing his wartime bit, Egypt was not on; or, as the politicians would say, it was not 'a viable option'.

So we moved to Blackpool, in March 1917. And in spite of the

War, and the fierce rationing (also normal), and the dark nights, and the sight of every other housewife wearing widow's weeds, it was for me an entry into paradise. For Blackpool was a luxury granted only once a year to the ordinary mortals of Lancashire. It was now to be my daily circus. Sand castles, and the sea, and the Pleasure Beach, and laying down lines on the sands at night for catching plaice, and ducking the high tides on the lower Promenade. A little later on, and in the crowded summertime, there was a special Sunday evening pleasure, all the more intense for being at once sinful and delayed. In those years, the Wesleyan Methodists held an overflow evening service in the Grand Theatre. By then, I was old enough to be an usher and hymn-book dispenser, a duty that relieved me from the compulsion to stay sitting through an interminable sermon. It was possible to hang around in the foyer and not even hear the man droning on with his promise of life eternal – for mill workers earning a pound a week. Such sociological ironies never crossed my mind in those callow youthful years, but I'm pretty sure that the younger bloods in the congregation were as impatient as I was for the blessed sound of the benediction, which was like a starting gun that sent two or three of us out along the Promenade and towards the sandhills (there were big rolling dunes then, both at the Squires Gate end and the North Shore) where you could get an eyeful of the promenading, and sometimes reclining, birds.

A Freudian item occurs to me here that may explain my later affection for all games both indoor and out. It was noticed by some concerned parson that as a small boy I played only with girls. (After adolescence it was, of course, big girls.) So at some point, care was taken that I should meet and play, for a change, with little boys. I took to marbles, then to flipping cigarette cards against the pavement, and then, when we moved to Blackpool, to fishing and cricket on the sands. And then to bagatelle. My father bought me a table for Christmas, a splendid thing of mahogany and green baize that I would gladly buy back today at its no doubt ruinously inflated price.

After that, though notorious from an early age for my addiction to books, I never felt any conflict between work and play. And so, in the course of time, and with my father's encouragement, I went on to play soccer, rugby, and cricket for the school; ping-pong, badminton, squash, tennis, you name it. But, for a happy period, between I should say the ages of eleven and fifteen, my particular mania was gymnastics. Next to the public library was the town gymnasium, and, since I lived up the road, I came at a tender age under the sharp eye and expert instruction of one H. Gregory, father of Alfred Gregory, the Alpinist. By the time I moved to the secondary school, as it then was, I was pretty good on the horizontal and parallel bars and had gone through the whole genteel gamut of country and folk dancing. During my years in the second and third forms, I must have been an odious figure to the giants of the Sixth. We had at the time a regular master who, until the sensible importation of H. Gregory himself, 'took' us at gym. He knew a few Swedish exercises and what he could recall of the army's routines. He was chronically fatigued and was always making excuses to skip his sessions with the Sixth. So he would get permission of the headmaster, a small bouncing figure of Roman imperiousness named J. Turral, to fork me out of my class (any class) in order to take the Sixth at gym. It must have been galling for those seventeen- and eighteen-year-olds, already sprouting the down of the first moustache, to have to obey the hip-hup instructions of a twelve-year-old, who now recalls with relish the mean pleasure of showing some hairy giant how to vault the pommel horse, perform handstands and cartwheels, not to mention the hopeless attempts to give them the elements of doing up-starts and 'hocks off' on the horizontal bar. I realised very much later why, for a time, I came in for a delinquent's share of 'lines' from the prefects, smarting under the helpless giggles of their contemporaries every time they demonstrated their ineptitude at climbing a rope or crashing from a handstand.

Football anyone? It took quite a while to get around to it, didn't it? But then it took me quite a while too. I had picked up from Hal Gregory a firm prejudice about the distinction between athletics and gymnastics. Athletics were for gorillas; gymnastics appealed to a subtler breed that appreciated grace and timing. After I had spent long Saturday afternoons at the gym, my father would come home from Bloomfield Road,* and pretty soon I was converted by his ravings about the speed of little Mee, the walloping defensive tactics of Tulloch, and the hair's-breadth retrieves of Mingay. I began to skip Saturday afternoons at the gym, except when we were in training with 'the girls' for the folk dancing division of the Lytham Festival. Of all those enchantresses I recall only one, because she was a knock-out and was the first girl to knock me flat.

So I became, with my father, a regular Bloomfield Roader. Of that 1920 team, I remember only Mee at outside-left, then Heathcote (who bore a surprising resemblance to Henry Edwards, the reigning British silent-screen star), Barrass with his curls, and Benton. The name of Donnachie has been suggested to me, but if he was there in my time he must have been on the injured list throughout the season. I'm also informed that Blackpool had a goalkeeper, around this time, by the name of Richardson. I am sorry to say he has left no impression on me. Mingay was the one, alternately the hero and the butt of the Bloomfield Road crowd. He was a glum little man with ping-pong-ball eyes, and lids as heavy as Sherlock Holmes got up as a Limehouse lascar. His regular expression was one of gloomy contempt for the game and the crowd. No footballer I remember, except possibly Harry Bedford, lurched so unpredictably, from one week to the next, between brilliance and bathos. One Saturday he fumbled everything; the next he slithered, darted, plunged, leapt, in a series of jagged but wonderful recoveries.

Bedford, of the permanently furrowed brow and the prison haircut, came to us, I guess, in 1921. He was, after Cecil Parkin, my sporting hero. And I watched him till the dizzy day he played for England. After that, the 'regulars' became hypercritical of

* Bloomfield Road was the home ground of Blackpool Football Club.

him, as Lancashire people will of anybody who has acquired an extra-local reputation and might begin to put on airs, which Bedford never did. I don't know if it's true of Lancashire crowds in general but the Bloomfield Road mob never lost its head over any idol. Either he was a 'reet champion' or he was 'disgoostin'.

I'm afraid my memories of Blackpool football fade after that, along with my enthusiasm. I played for the secondary school and cannot truthfully say I was crazy about standing between the goalposts on witheringly dank afternoons. Then the inimitable J. Turral, who was a terrible snob but an absolutely Dickensian original, decided that soccer was gross, fit only for cave dwellers. So the school changed over to rugby, and I didn't enjoy that much either, breaking my back and weaning arthritis in the mud on other shivery Saturdays, as I heeled the ball out to Ken Jones or Norman Hinton.

When I went to Cambridge, I swore never to play football again, and I never did. There was, astoundingly, no gymnasium at Cambridge, so for a brief spell I turned to long jumping. I had the honour of jumping for Jesus (the college, not the Superstar) but, since sport was no longer compulsory, I gave it up, what with the humid, steaming Fen country and the jolt to the system of thudding your heels in the sand-pit twice a week.

Years later, by the time I'd become the New Yorker guide-in-residence to visiting Englishmen, I would incite them to watch American football because it was, and is, such a fascinating combination of chess and armoured warfare. But I always warned them that they might take understandable offence at the nauseating American habit of using substitutes every time a man bruised an ankle; and the even more odious custom of bounding to embrace each other after every touchdown. Well, two years ago, I saw my first English soccer match in decades and, sure enough, the players had followed the usual English procedure of first ridiculing an American fashion and then adopting and exaggerating it. To watch any soccer player in the moment after he has socked the ball into the net would give a man from Mars the impression that he was seeing a film clip of VE Day or the arrival of Lindbergh at Le Bourget.

Since my family died, I have not been back to Blackpool. But on the last trips, I had a regular sensation, as the train wheeled around the coastline and the Tower came into view, that I had never known in all the years I lived in Blackpool or travelled there. In the interval between the Bloomfield Road days and my last few visits to my ageing mother, I had taken up golf in the most maniacal way. Being still incapable of keeping books and sport apart, I read everything I could find on the game. And now, some years later, I regard myself as having earned a creditable Master's degree in the history of golf. On the last visits, when the train gave the lurch that takes it alongside the green undulations of Royal Lytham & St Annes, I got up and dropped the window and peered out. This was the very place where Robert Tyre Jones, the immortal one, and all the more immortal now that he is dead, fired his devastating iron shot from a bunker or sandy swale on the seventeenth to win the British Open of 1926 and obliterate Al Watrous.* On that very day, I was four miles away, playing cricket amid the yeasty odours of the abattoir that adjoined the Secondary School field. How dull, blind, and insensitive can a boy be?!

---

* Albert (Al) Watrous (1899–1983): American professional golfer who played on the PGA Tour and the Senior PGA Tour. He was in the 1927 and 1929 Ryder Cup team and was the club pro at Oakland Hills CC in Michigan for 37 years.

3

Goodbye, Mr President,
Hi There, Arnie!

1968

A friend of mine who has been, he tells me, a notable golf writer for twenty years or so once made the mistake of putting himself down as 'golf correspondent' on the routine immigration card you fill out when you enter France. He was immediately held for questioning. There was nothing particularly sinister about his appearance (baggy suit, suede shoes, a Royal & Ancient tie). It was simply that the French had never seen a 'golf correspondent' before, and when it was explained to them that there are people who travel the world in order to describe how many blows it takes a man to knock a little white ball into eighteen gopher holes, they were curious to examine the mental processes of such a freak.

Until only a year or two ago, this would have been my reaction. I also shared H. L. Mencken's view of golfers: 'If I had my way, any man guilty of golf would be ineligible for any public office or trust in these United States, and the females of the breed would be shipped off to the white-slave corrals of the Argentine.' But my lifelong purity was defiled in a single afternoon in late June 1964 when, at the urging of a superficially decent Englishman, I was taken out with a bag of oddly shaped sticks to fumble around Van Cortlandt Park, the oldest public course in or near New York, in 168 swipes. (I believe my record still stands.)

Any self-respecting man would have stopped right there. But I was, and am, the product of a Methodist upbringing. And while any normal sinner can take or leave his vices, it is fatal to introduce a Methodist to a whiff of sin. He was trained on many a Sunday afternoon to believe that one puff on a cigarette behind the barn is the certain prescription for life in a sanatorium, that after a single sniff of a beer bottle he will desert his wife, auction his children and expire in the gutters of the Bowery. Show him a lipstick ad and he is ready for every perversion in the Kraft-Ebbing and Andy Warhol catalogues. It takes a practised sinner to practise moderation. The good boy should avoid the first drop.

The narcotics experts define a true narcotic as one that produces a recurring chemical cycle of desire. Well, sir, it took only a trembling week or two for the Van Cortlandt Itch to seize me again. Knowing full well that I was doing wrong, I was yet led out like a zombie by the same specious Englishman (my connection, I guess you could call him) to buy a set of clubs. Once more I floundered and lashed around a course. Then I made a fatal decision. If I was going to become an addict, I would find me some Timothy Leary who could teach me how to regulate the trips. I had 'picked up' tennis as a boy, and wasn't bad and wasn't good either. At the age of twenty-seven, I took three lessons from Suzanne Lenglen's pro and abandoned the game for ever. I had learned enough to confirm my suspicion that the 'natural' way of playing a game is the worst way. All fine gamesmen learn to do the unnatural thing in a natural way. God knows, no movement in the whole of golf was inspired by nature, as the professionals' chronic bursas, ripped trapezius muscles and twisted sacroiliacs will testify. So a month to the day of my first lapse, I phoned the golf club nearest to my house at the end of Long Island. I enquired if they had a pro. They had. I fixed a fix for the following day at ten o'clock. I appeared. A small blond barrel of a man, crowding seventy, took me out to a bit of pasture. 'What,' he said, 'seems to be the trouble?'

'No trouble,' I said, 'except I'd like to know which end you hit with.'

(This, I was later to learn, was not so idiotic as it sounds. Most of the best players hit with the top of the shaft. Phil

Galvano recommends using the wrist watch. Judge 'Ike' Handy dispenses with the club altogether; once he has swung it back he leaves the clubhead 'up there' and swings his hands. To tell the truth, my own most successful rounds have been played without clubs, ball or course. I find I can retain the most reliable, and often superb, control by simply lying down, closing both eyes and keeping the head very still on a pillow.)

The small blond barrel gave me a short, sharp look, realised that I was newly hooked and no joker, and said: 'All right, then, take out a 7-iron and let's see what happens.' We have been seeing what happens ever since. By wonderful good luck, the blond barrel turned out to be George Heron, who started at the age of eleven making clubs for Vardon, who for thirty-eight years was the Meadowbrook pro, and who has often been summoned in time of need to the bedside of the giants of the game. He is now retired, happily four miles from where I live. Under his patient care, I have become in the space of three years as fine an example as I have seen of the fairway spastic, that is to say a man who in practice hits effortless shots of heartbreaking beauty which then evade him from the first tee to the nineteenth, where mysteriously the beauty and the skill reappear again. Anyway, I did sneak up to Van Cortlandt last fall and precisely halved the original record. And next season is going to be quite different.

My only qualification for writing about the marvellous mania is, therefore, that I have been majoring in golf for over three years and may be in time to deter some other intending addict. I have been a foreign correspondent for thirty years, but for the past three years shelves of books on diplomacy, the corn–hog ratio, the CIA and Ronald Reagan have been shovelled into a closet to make way for the sturdy American eagles that enclose the works of Hogan, Hagen, Snead, Galvano, Jenkins, Boros, Price and Wind, Cotton, Boomer, Handy, Armour, Longhurst, Darwin, Jones and Jones. Ward-Thomas and Dante (Jim, that is) are in there too, even though they don't scan.

Because I am a journalist, I naturally fell in with the cagey breed of golf writers, who have never done a lick of work in their lives but amble around the countryside sneering at Snead and picking Cotton apart. It was through two of the most engaging of these bounders that I was led off the practice tee and into the strange world of golf, where the Anglo-Saxon still reigns supreme, where 18th-century servants known as 'caddies' defer to their masters, where never is heard a discouraging word about such trifles as Vietnam, or the coming doomsday of the cities, and where the journalist is a tolerated bum. But not, it seems, in England. There the 'golf correspondent's' relation to the emperors of the game is not unlike that of Mr Watson to Sherlock Holmes or Rasputin to Nicholas the Second.

I was fortunate to be introduced to the English game by Pat Ward-Thomas, the *Guardian*'s man, who gave me my first glimpse of a tournament anywhere at the Piccadilly [World Match Play at Wentworth] in 1966 (Chapter 17). My first glimpse of Heaven was at Augusta last April, when Herbert Warren Wind* played St Peter.

It was during the memorable week of the last Masters that I learned in an evening how much more awesome was the world of golf than the world of politics. One morning Ward-Thomas terrified me by saying, in the most off-hand way, that he had arranged an evening date with his pal Arnold Palmer. For this ordeal, I discarded the roguish Stinchfield slacks I had bought in Palm Beach and the camel's hair cardigan from the Burlington Arcade. I bathed for half an hour, like a pilgrim preparing himself for Mecca. I laid out the black suit, the pearly white shirt with the Kent collar and the New Delhi Tiger Club tie which I normally reserve for evenings at Baden-Baden or Roseland. When I was fully costumed and shaking slightly I joined Ward-Thomas in the car.

'Good God, man!' he croaked, 'what are you got up like that for?'

---

* Herbert Warren Wind, the only writer to win the USGA's Bob Jones Award, died in 2005, aged 88. He contributed to the *New Yorker* and *Sports Illustrated* and also wrote fourteen books.

'We are going to visit the Palmers, aren't we?'

'One would think,' he mocked, 'you were going to see the President of the United States.'

'The President!' I screamed, 'if I were off to see old Elbie Jay, I'd more likely be dressed like you.'

Ward-Thomas was himself in the British sports writer's invariable party costume of voluminous soup-stained slacks, a blue shirt (which serves as sports shirt by day, pyjama top by night) and a threadbare sports coat impressed with decaying hound's teeth. This is not a careless outfit; it is a rather cunning ploy used by Englishmen who are running a little short on invitations. It invokes instant sympathy in warm-hearted Americans and a rush of drinks and offers to convalesce in country houses. It is thus a kind of portable prop.

It is not true that I would appear at the White House in anything so sordid or calculated. But the Roosevelts, Trumans, Churchills, Eisenhowers, Kennedys and Johnsons had been the pros of my working life for a quarter of a century and I had been with them all on occasions so informal, or desperate, that lending a clean shirt to a campaign-weary Kennedy, sharing a six-passenger spare rib at the ole ranch, helping Stevenson out of a cowboy's outfit at the Merced County fair were the normal hazards of my trade. I don't remember dolling up for an hour with Nehru and as a matter of fact I made a point of dressing as much like Ward-Thomas as possible, to indicate contempt, on a visit to Hitler in the Braunhaus. 'But Palmer ...' I said. What sort of an oaf did the oafish Ward-Thomas think I was?

He got lost in the dark boulevards of night-time Augusta, and I half-hoped he would miss the house. I did not feel up to this peasant's intrusion on the Emperor. However, we found the house. Palmer was dressed in an American variation of Ward-Thomas, and he had in one or two of his court. They all could have passed for unemployed gas-station attendants. But the great man never faltered. He took me in without a hint that I was a social pariah. I might have been 'family' late for Thanksgiving. Mrs Palmer was as gracious as Mrs Coolidge receiving the Tibetan ambassador. Next year, I felt, with a few more strokes off my handicap, I could relax into at least non-matching coat and pants.

A year on who knows, I might even jump into blue jeans and screw up my courage to call on Nicklaus (the first).

4

Bobby Jones – The Gentleman from Georgia

1999

Jones, Robert Tyre Jr. Lawyer, engineer, scholar, amateur golfer.

b. March 17, 1902. Son of Robert Tyre Jones, lawyer. For first five years was enfeebled by a puzzling disease, but at age six, won Atlanta East Lake Club's children's championship. At fourteen, was Georgia amateur champion and went through to quarter-final of US Amateur championship. In following two years, won Southern amateur. Throughout 1918, the sixteen-year-old toured in exhibition matches on behalf of the Red Cross and War Relief.

Ed. Public schools of Atlanta till age of fifteen, when he entered Georgia Institute of Technology. Graduated three years later with degree in mechanical engineering. At age eighteen, in 1920, began to enter open golf championships, and continued to play in them for next eight years, during the summer vacations from his studies. 1923, honours degree in English literature, Harvard; won his first US Open championship. After a brief fling at real estate, in 1926 he entered Emory University Law School and after three semesters passed Georgia bar examination. He consequently withdrew and set up law practice, which he maintained for most of his life. He was essentially a weekend golfer, in the fall and the spring. In 1924 he married Mary Rice Malone, of Atlanta. They had three children.

Between 1923 and 1930, Jones entered twenty major championships, won thirteen and came second in four. During that time, the leading two professionals of the day, Walter Hagen and Gene Sarazen,* never won a British or United States Open that Jones entered. In eight years of Walker Cup competition, he won all his singles matches. In the summer of 1930, he won in succession the US Open, the British Open, the British Amateur and the US Amateur, subsequently called 'the Grand Slam', a feat never performed before or since. Jones thereupon retired from competitive golf at the age of twenty-eight. In 1930, a group of friends purchased an abandoned southern nursery, which had served as the fruit farm for the Confederate armies. On these 360 acres, Jones, with the help of Scottish architect Dr Alister Mackenzie, designed the Augusta National golf course. With financier Clifford Roberts, he founded the Augusta National Golf Club and a Jones's invitational tournament, later called (against Jones's wish) the Masters.

In the Second World War, although deferred as a forty-year-old father of three and suffering a medical disability, he was commissioned in Army Air Force intelligence and served in Europe under Eisenhower's command. In 1948, a painful back compelled him to give up golf. After two operations, he was diagnosed with a rare degenerative disease, which progressively paralysed him. In 1958, he was given the freedom of the city (burgh) of St Andrews, Scotland. He died in Atlanta, in December 1971.

On the centennial of the birth of Mr Justice Holmes, I was asked to write a commemorative piece for a liberal weekly. By that time, his reputation as a liberal hero was as secure as Jane Austen's new reputation as a pioneer feminist, an elevation that, if she were within earshot, would – as she might say – 'vastly astound' her. Holmes had been so exhaustively written about, so firmly established as the Great Dissenter, that there seemed very

* For Walter Hagen see Chapter 9. Gene Sarazen (1902–1999): Won seven Majors, played in six US Ryder Cup teams. From 1984 till 1999 played the honorary opening tee shot at the Masters in company with Byron Nelson and Sam Snead.

little to say about him. I accordingly said very little and summed it all up in the title of the piece: 'What Have We Left for Mr Justice Holmes?' It took many years, and the leisure to look him over freed from his obituary pigeonhole, to make the alarming discovery that the cases in which he voted with the conservative majority as against it were in the ratio of eight or ten to one; and that two notable scholars succeeded each other in spending years preparing his biography only to abandon it to a third man who saw what they had seen in Holmes, but one who also had the courage to say it out loud: that Holmes's political philosophy was (his concern for free speech apart) as fine an intellectual approximation to Fascism as you would care to find among the savants of the Western world.

I have come to a similar hurdle with Robert Tyre Jones Jr, though one nothing like so formidable or alarming. I don't suppose any other athletic hero, certainly no one in golf, has been written about so often and with so much reverence. The same admirable anecdotes are repeated whenever his name is mentioned: his debunking of the teaching clichés ('never up, never in'); his famous putdown by Harry Vardon ('did you ever see a worse shot than that?'); his identifying the enemy as 'Old Man Par'; his calling a two-stroke penalty on himself to lose a championship ('you might as well praise a man for not robbing a bank'). And on and on. I have heard these stories a hundred times and concluded long ago that fresh anecdotes about Jones are as few and far between as new funny golf stories. This must be, then, a small memoir of a short friendship in the last years of his life and what I gleaned about him and his character.

In the summer of 1965, when I had been for nearly twenty years the chief American correspondent of the (then *Manchester*) *Guardian*, our golf correspondent, Pat Ward-Thomas, for some reason or other was unable to cover the US Open championship, which was being held, I believe for the first time, at Creve Coeur in St Louis. I filled in for him and my last day's dispatch eventually appeared in the *Guardian*'s annual anthology of the paper's writing. Somehow, a copy of it got to Jones. He wrote me a letter saying, as I recall, he was unaware that 'golf was another string to your bow'. Why he should have known anything about my 'bow' was news to me. But he mentioned that he had been a regular viewer of *Omnibus*, a ninety-minute network television potpourri of drama, science, politics, history, ballet, and God knows what, which I hosted in the 1950s. Jones's letter was, of course, highly flattering to me, especially since this was the first piece I had ever written about golf [Chapter 16]. I had taken up the game only one year before, at an advanced age (in my mid-fifties – hopeless, I know); but, being a journalist, I started to write about it, just as when you run into a man who is an expert on the manufacture of heels for ladies' shoes – as was a man I met in Rainelle, West Virginia – you write about him.

There was another short exchange or two, in one of which Jones characteristically started a letter: 'Dear Alistair (don't you think we ought to put an end to this minuet of Mr Jones and Mr Cooke?)' and went on to ask me to be sure to call on him whenever I was down in Augusta or Atlanta. Which I did, most often in the company of Ward-Thomas.

My first impression was the shock of seeing the extent of his disability, the fine strong hands, twisted like the branches of a cypress, gamely clutching a tumbler or one of his perpetual cigarettes in a holder. His face was more ravaged than I had expected, from the long-endured pain I imagine, but the embarrassment a stranger might feel about this was tempered by the quizzical eyes and the warmth his presence gave off. (He kept on going to Augusta for the Masters until two years before the end. Mercifully, for everyone but his family, we would not see him when he could no longer bear to be seen.)

After that first meeting I never again felt uncomfortable about his ailment, and only once did he mention it, which was when he spoke a sentence that has passed into the apocrypha. Pat well knew that Jones never talked about his disease, but on that day he really wanted to penetrate the mask of courage and know just how good or bad things really were. Pat's expression was so candid that – I sensed – Jones felt he would, for once, say a word or two. He said that he'd been told that his disease occurred in two forms – 'descending and ascending', that luckily his paralysis had been from the waist and his extremities down, so that, he added, 'I have my heart and lungs and my so-called brain'. He spoke about it easily with a rueful smile, and no more was said. The familiar punch line, 'You know, we play the ball where it lies,' was not said in my presence and, I must say, it sounds to me false to Jones's character, as of a passing thought by a screenwriter that Hollywood would never resist. Let us thank God that Hollywood has never made a movie about Jones; it would almost surely be as inept and more molassic than the dreadful *Follow the Sun*, the alleged 'epic' about Ben Hogan.

About the disease. At a tournament Jones was playing in, in England, Henry Longhurst, the late, great rogue of English golf writing (see Chapter 27), was standing beside a doctor who, marvelling at Jones's huge pivot, the long arc of his swing and the consequent muscular strain that sustained it, predicted that one day it would cause him grievous back trouble. Longhurst wrote and retailed this comment to Jones, who responded with a good-tempered note saying, with typical tact, that Henry was good to be concerned but the trouble was due to a rare disease. This sad turn in Jones's life has also received several versions. So far as I can discover, from tapping the memory of his oldest surviving friend, the inimitable Charlie Yates, and checking with the expertise of several medicos, the true account is simple and drastic.

In the summer of 1948, Jones remarked to Yates, in the middle of what was to be his last round ever, that he would not soon be playing again because his back had become unbearable and he was going to have an operation. It was, in fact, the first of two operations and it revealed damage to the spinal tissue that could not then be tagged with a definite diagnosis. A year or two later, Jones went up to Boston and, after being examined at the Lahey Clinic, had the second operation, during which a positive diagnosis was made: syringomyelia, a chronic progressive degenerative disease of the spinal cord, which, as we all know, Jones bore for twenty-two years with chilling stoicism. The scant consolation for the rest of us is that anyone falling victim to the same disease today could expect no better outcome. The aetiology is still unknown and there is no cure.

When I first went into the sitting room of Jones's cottage at Augusta, I noticed at once a large picture over the mantelpiece, a framed series of cartoon strips by the best, and throughout the 1920s and 1930s, the most famously popular English sports cartoonist, Tom Webster. No American I knew (and no Englishman under seventy) had ever heard his name, but the drawings – of Jones and of Hagen, I believe – served as a taproot into Jones's memories of Britain and British golf in the 1920s. He enlightened me about the character and skill of various old heroes I brought up: Braid and Duncan and Tolley and Roger Wethered* and, of course, Hagen. (Though I played no golf I followed it – from the papers, the newsreels, and the Webster cartoons – as zealously as I followed county cricket.) This talk brought up, one time, the never-ending controversy about the essential characteristic of the good golf swing. Jones distrusted 'keep your eye on the ball' almost as much as Tommy Armour did. His preference was for Abe Mitchell's 'the player should move freely beneath himself'.

Jones never recalled to me, as all famous athletes are apt to do, the acclaim of his great days, though once when I had just come back from St Andrews, he remarked again what a 'wonderful experience' it had been on his later visits 'to go about a town where people wave at you from doorways and windows'. Otherwise, he never said anything that made me doubt his friends' assurance that he was uncomfortable with the spotlight and was grateful to have room service in the hotels of towns

---

* All British golfers in the early twentieth century. James Braid won five Open Championships; George Duncan won the Open in 1920, the first to be played following the First World War; Cyril Tolley was British Amateur champion in 1920 and 1929 and represented Great Britain in the Walker Cup six times. Roger Wethered was runner-up in the 1921 Open, British Amateur champion in 1923 and played in the Walker Cup five times.

where he would be recognised on the streets. He did not flaunt his trophies at home, and he kept his medals locked up in a chest.

Our talks were mostly about books, people, politics, only rarely about golf, whenever Ward-Thomas was eager for another Jones quote for his bulging file of golfing wisdom. In the winter after my first meeting, a book came out entitled *Bobby Jones on Golf*, and I reviewed it under the heading 'The Missing Aristotle Papers on Golf' [Chapter 5], remarking along the way that Jones's gift for distilling a complex emotion into the barest language would not have shamed John Donne; that his meticulous insistence on the right word to impress the right visual image was worthy of fussy old Flaubert; and that his unique personal gift was 'to take apart many of the club clichés with a touch of grim Lippmannesque humour'. Shortly after the piece appeared, Jones dropped me a letter beginning: 'Offhand, I can't think of another contemporary author who has been compared in one piece to Aristotle, Flaubert, John Donne and Walter Lippmann!'

Much was made – rightly – when the book came out about the extraordinary fact that Jones had written it himself. This is only to remark, in a more interesting way, how phenomenally rare it is for a scholar to become a world-class athlete. The same dependence on a ghost is true of actors and actresses, as also of ninety per cent of the world's – at least the Western world's – best politicians. The exceptions are rare indeed. Churchill, after a Washington wartime meeting with Roosevelt, flew home in a bomber, alternating between the controls and the composition of a speech on a pad. He was no sooner in London than he appeared at the BBC and broadcast across the Atlantic a majestic strategical survey of the world at war. To his horror, Roosevelt heard it in the White House while he was working on his own promised broadcast with the aid of three ghost-writers. One of them, Robert Sherwood, consoled the president with the sorrowful thought: 'I'm afraid, Mr President, he rolls his own.'

When I think back to those Augusta talks, I recall most vividly the quality of irony that was always there in his eyes and often in his comments on people and things. I asked him once about 'the master eye' without knowing that he had written about it. I'm sure he said what he had said before: he didn't believe in it or in the ritual of plumb bobbing.* The main thing was to 'locate the ball's position ... I'm told a man can do this better with two eyes than with one'. The last time I saw him, I told him about a rather morose Scottish caddie I'd recently had who took a dim view of most things American, but especially the golf courses, which – he'd been told – had lots of trees. We were sitting out on the porch of his Augusta cottage and Jones looked down at the towering Georgia pines, the great cathedral nave, of the plunging tenth fairway. 'I don't see,' he said deadpan, 'any need for a tree on a golf course.'

Towards the end of one Masters tournament, Henry Longhurst took suddenly very ill. He lay grumpily in his hospital bed and, lifting his ripe W. C. Fields's nose over the bed sheet, predicted that it was 'closing time'. Happily, it turned out not to be, but Pat and I stayed over through the Monday to watch out for him. In the early afternoon, when the place was empty, we called on Jones and he suggested we collect some clubs from the pro shop and play the splendid par three course. We were about to set off when Cliff Roberts, cofounder of the club, came in. He was shocked at the generosity of Jones's suggestion: 'Bob, you surely know the rule – no one can play without a member going along.' 'Don't you think,' Jones asked wistfully, 'you and I could exercise a little Papal indulgence?' Roberts did not think so. And although he'd recently had a major operation, he went off, got into his golfing togs and limped around with us through six holes, by which time he was ready for intensive care and staggered away accepting the horrid fact of the broken rule.

Because of the firm convention of writing nothing about Jones that is less than idolatrous, I have done a little digging among friends and old golfing acquaintances who knew him and among

* Plumb bobbing: a method of reading putts where the player generally squats and dangles the putter (head down) from the fingers (like a surveyor's plumb line) in front of him to check the line to the hole.

old and new writers who, in other fields, have a sharp nose for the disreputable. But I do believe that a whole team of investigative reporters, working in shifts like coal miners, would find that in all of Jones's life anyone had been able to observe, he nothing common did or mean.

However, a recent author, in a book depicting the Augusta National Golf Club as a CEO's Shangri-la, does not spare the patron saint of golf from his lamentations. He attacks Jones on two counts. First, for his being 'weak and irresolute' in bowing to Cliff Roberts's expulsion of a player for violating the etiquette of the game. (On the contrary, Jones was disturbed by the man's behaviour for six years. Only when, after three requests, the man properly apologised, did Jones welcome him back.) This criticism reflects a serious misconception about Jones's function. In the running of the Masters, Cliff Roberts's power was absolute. What Jones brought to the tournament was the prestige of his immense popularity, not to mention a saving contribution of seed money when the club was on the verge of foundering. Otherwise, it was understood from the start that Roberts was the prime mover and shaker, the organiser of the staff and the commissary, the recruiter and commander of the course patrols, the boss of the course officials and of crowd control, the inventor of new conventions of scoring, and even (over Jones's protesting pleas) the final judge of the architecture of a hole.

So the view of Jones as the impotent puppet king of a cabal of CEOs is both melodramatic and quite wrong. In the beginning, Jones and Roberts wrote to hundreds of friends, acquaintances and strangers 'to buy a share of the club' but recruited only a minuscule membership; a hundred dollars a head was hard to come by in the pit of the Depression. Incidentally, the slur also blandly ignores the deepening agony of Jones's illness throughout the last twenty years of his attendance at 'his' tournament. (His private view of the tycoon's preserve that Augusta was to become was never, I believe, vouchsafed to his friends, but it was after a hearty get-together of board chairmen, celebrated in a photo opportunity more theirs than his, that he confided ruefully: 'They say I love people. I don't. I love a few people in small doses.')

The second charge is more familiar and these days has become inevitable when a young author reacts to warm praise of an old southerner. It is the charge of 'racism'. This is so pretentiously silly that I have to swallow hard to choose to meet it. It is the old fallacy, which every generation is subject to, of judging a man outside his time and place. Franklin Roosevelt now, I imagine, is thought in retrospect to have had a very callous streak since he never protested the separation of the races. Many shocked readers of this piece would have felt the same indifference if they had been born a half century earlier. I know. I was there. During my first two years in America, I was curious about, but not outraged by, the social status of the Negroes. In my most enlightened moments I should have thought of them as an aberration in an otherwise admirable system. The Negro was not yet a crusade, even among bloodshot liberals.

I look back on the southerners I knew and admired. I was lucky to have travelled far and wide in the South in the 1930s and 1940s, and I had many friends in many southern places. Jones belonged to those fine ones who were incapable of condescending to a black or being ever less than conscious of their lowly status. When things went wrong for their servants – sickness, debt, delinquency – the family took anxious care of them, of its own. By contrast, we in the North hired daily help in good conscience and hoped they stayed well. Their private afflictions were their own. The northern Negro might be permitted more public chutzpah than his southern brother, but the North took it out in tuberculosis.

For myself, I can now say simply that in my life I can count four human beings who radiated simple goodness: my father; a Franciscan priest; a university professor; and Robert Tyre Jones Jr. Maybe 'radiated' is too strong a word, for one striking thing about good human beings is their gift for not being striking. Jones had an instinct for noticing, and attending to, the shy one in any bubbling company. His capacity for shifting the spotlight away from himself was remarkable even in the one performance where you would expect him to be authoritative: in the act of teaching golf. In those precious film shorts he made for the Warner brothers, in which a lesson in the use of the brassie* or mashie† is tagged on to a ludicrous plot about a golf widow or other domestic strain, he never says, 'you must do this . . .' or 'it is essential to do that'. He is careful always to say: 'I've found that if I move the ball an inch or so . . .' and 'perhaps if you tried . . . it works well with some people'.

The last indelible memory of him, for those who had the luck to be in St Andrews in the late autumn of 1958, was his acceptance of the freedom of the city. The Provost was careful to say that he was being saluted not only as 'the first golfer of this age . . . but as a man of courage and character'. In response, Jones put aside the notes he had painfully written out and spoke freely, first of the Old Course, which had enraged the nineteen-year-old and come to enchant the man; then he talked with the slightest tremor of the curious lasting friendship he had acquired for a city and a people 'who have a sensitivity and an ability to extend cordiality in ingenious ways'.

He hobbled off to his electric golf cart and began to propel it down the centre aisle, as the audience stirred, picked up the cue of a tentative voice, and rose to sing 'Will Ye No' Come Back Again?' The start of the hobble and the fact of the cart were enough to remind them that he never would. It was a moment of suddenly shared emotion that upset the most cynical. Herbert Warren Wind remarked: 'It was ten minutes before many who attended were able to speak with a tranquil voice.' During those minutes, he seemed to one onlooker to qualify for Frederick Buechner's definition of goodness as 'valour and unnatural virtue'.

What we are left with in the end is a forever young, good-looking southerner, an impeccably courteous and decent man

---

* Brassie: a 2-wood, so named because the clubhead was originally faced with brass.
† Mashie (niblick): a lofted iron used for medium distances, similar to a present-day 7-iron.

with a private ironical view of life who, to the great good fortune of people who saw him, happened to play the great game with more magic and more grace than anyone before or since.

5

The Missing Aristotle
Papers on Golf*

1967

The current *Golf Digest* lists thirty-eight books of instruction.
Through the northern winter hundreds of thousands of slaves
to the marvellous mania will be thrashing on their pillows
imagining themselves chanting *Swing Easy, Hit Hard* with Julius
Boros and *Never Say Never* with Bobby Nichols, rehearsing the
tricks of *Chipping and Putting* with Billy Casper, snatching
the *Secret of Holing Putts* from Horton Smith or the *Secrets
of the Perfect Golf Swing* from Phil Galvano, and yielding at last
to the sure-fire sedative of *My 55 Ways to Lower Your Golf
Score* by Jack Nicklaus. Over breakfast, there will be the cartoon
'tips' of Palmer, Snead, and Tommy Armour. And once a month,
the golf magazines will rush through the mails the absolutely
final word on retarding the right side, swinging the hands,
sliding the hips, forgetting the hips, eliminating sway, tension,
casting, steering, scooping, slicing, hooking, the loose grip, the
tight grip, the flat swing, the upright swing, the lot.

Anyone who has laboured over the literature and then discovered how reluctant the human body is to see the word made
flesh is bound to conclude sooner or later that the trouble
with the books is that they are mostly written by men who play
great golf and write duffer prose. It is true, of course, that
practically every book that carries the by-line of a champ was
ghosted; 'the authors,' as Charles Price puts it, 'had as much

* A review of *Bobby Jones on Golf*, by Robert Tyre (Bobby) Jones, Doubleday,
New York, 1966.

to do with the actual writing of them as King James did with writing the Holy Bible'.

This is where the failure, and the frustration, set in. The self-effacing ghost, at his most conscientious, sits and argues with the King for days and months and then tries to set down what he thinks the great man means. The big question is, does the great man know what he does so wonderfully? For the raw material they both have to master is not golf but the communication of feelings so fine that they could only be perfectly conveyed by somebody able to handle great complexity of emotion in the barest prose. Donne, thou shouldst be slicing at this hour! At one end of the golf library, you have Ben Hogan analysing a split-second motion as a compressed course in aerodynamics. At the other end, you have Snead, the happy hillbilly, saying, 'Step up to that little ball like you're going to love it, keep saying "you little sweet thing, I'm not going to hurt you".' With the closest attention to these masters, the learner steps to the ball and ends up with only one sure feeling, that of baffled admiration for the fact that Hogan fired balls more precisely than anyone who ever played, and that Snead at fifty-four, in spite of his instructions, still swings the most graceful club in the game.

And now, in anticipation akin to reverence, the learner can take up, surprisingly, the only book entirely devoted to golf instruction to be put out by the immortal one himself. Between 1927 and 1935, Jones wrote two columns a week for a syndicate, which Charles Price has splendidly salvaged and distilled to about one-fifth of the original bulk. He handed the manuscript over to Jones for his approval. Whereupon, to Price's amazement, and our gratitude, the author then 'picked apart every chapter, every paragraph, every sentence, every phrase of his own writing until he was sure that thirty years had not dimmed what he truly meant to say'.

So what we have is a unique manual. One of the handful of very great golfers is also revealed as a literate and intensely thoughtful man who modestly shares the agony of Flaubert: to re-experience a feeling and transmit it with exactness to another person. In other words, unlike the vast majority of golfers, he knows precisely what he is doing. Unlike any other before him, he can say what he is doing.

It comes down, I think, to the business of metaphor, especially to the intense form of it embodied in an idiom. Whether a man learns golf from a pro or a book, or supplements one with the other, he is trying to impress on his visual memory, and then on his muscular habits, a series of metaphors designed by the great ones to give him the 'feel' of the swing. Linking only the favourite images of, say, Percy Boomer, Snead, Lema, Hogan, and Galvano, he will arrive at this astonishing picture: of a man standing in a barrel, his arms hanging down like an ape's, about to clasp his hands around a bird, too tight to let it go but not tight enough to hurt it. Pretty soon, he is swivelling to the right in the barrel and finds that his left arm has mysteriously fused into the line of the shaft, which he now uses to describe an arc. At the top of the back swing, he tries to point his left thumb at his right ear, which is quite a trick since he is also intent on carrying a tray with his right hand. At last he swivels back, does a lateral shimmy with his hips and then attempts, according to taste, either to pull down on a bell rope, or thresh a field of wheat, or hit the ball with his wristwatch or plant the top of the shaft in the ground.

Most players have heard of these images and for most of us some of them transfer their meaning with great effect and others mean nothing at all. A good deal of the bickering that goes on among the great pros is not so much due to their differing on essentials as to the other guy's metaphor seeming forced or unreal.

It is the great gift of Bobby Jones that, in analysing all the motions from 'holding the club' to 'the competitive attitude', he is acutely aware that 'the words in our language that we must use to describe feel are necessarily vague and susceptible to varying interpretations among different persons ... for this reason I think it is necessary in all forms of golf instruction to repeat over and over descriptions of the same movements, all the while altering the modes of expression and terms of reference'. So there is no shibboleth too familiar to escape his painstaking probe. He dislikes 'keeping your eye on the ball' and prefers 'staying behind it', or – better – Abe Mitchell's saying that 'the player should move freely beneath himself'. Many of the club clichés he takes apart with a touch of grim, Lippmannesque humour. (On 'never up, never in': 'Of course, we never know but that the ball which is on line and stops short would have holed out. But we *do* know that the ball that ran past did not hole out.') He discovered, after many playing years, that 'hitting from the inside' could be felt more vividly if he thought of trying to swing the club 'through the ball outward toward the right edge of the fairway'. For the first time, the universal misunderstanding implicit in the advice to establish the left arm as a continuation of the shaft is exposed in the Aristotelian sentence: 'The teaching that the left arm and the club should lie in the same vertical plane is all right, but no one in his wildest moments ever conceived that they should lie in the same plane *in any other* direction.'

Here is no Boomer testiness ('you are by no means trying to hit the ball'), no Armour bullying, no 'tips', no dogma, and – thank God – no locker-room humour. Here is the fruit of fifty years' observation of golf by the wariest intelligence and the most attractive man who has ever played the game greatly. As such, it is the classic manual and a boon to the learner and, I am told, the expert alike.

6

Robert Tyre Jones Jr,
What Won the Grand Slam?

2000

The popular memory of every great athlete is a romantic mixture of the truth and spectacular legend. Babe Ruth not only scored more homers than anybody, he could hit the stadium clock face whenever he chose to. Mark Spitz could swim the turn-around length in record time, too. Jesse Owens could outrun a horse.

The legend of Bobby Jones's Grand Slam is that in one magical summer, in 1930, by playing his incomparable best this amateur beat all comers both amateur and professional, at a time when the best amateurs were as good as the best pros; and that, by winning all four majors in one year, he established himself as the wonder man of golf.

The truth contains little magic and only one round of high drama. But succeeding generations who never saw him simply look back in awe. Nobody has explained what really happened, and how Jones managed what had never been done before and has never been done since. Nobody, that is, except Jones himself. The key to his extraordinary feat lies buried in Jones's own writings: his reminiscences (*Golf is My Game*) and the collection of essays which form a teaching manual (*Bobby Jones on Golf*). Together they constitute a unique record, since Jones was not only the best player of his time but the most thoughtful writer on the game of any time. Consequently, although he himself never attempts an outright explanation, his two books offer a body of evidence in such revealing detail that it is possible to deduce not Who Done It but What Did It.

He carefully recites the conditions of play (from a gale at St Andrews to 'the hottest day I can ever remember' at Inter-lachen); the day-by-day pace of the greens; the character of his opponent in every round; the rise and fall of his fortunes through the crucial matches; most significantly, the astonishing con-fession that only on the last leg of the Slam, in the last match at Merion, was he at the peak of his game. He tells a brutal anecdote that opens up this mystery.

After he had won both the British Amateur and the British Open, he sailed home to prepare first for the US Open in Minnesota. On the boat train to Southampton, Jones and his wife had along as a travelling companion Cyril Tolley, the most formidable, if not the most tactful, of Jones's British opponents. 'Bob,' drawled Tolley, 'how long have you been over here?' About six weeks, Jones replied. 'Do you suppose,' mused Tolley, 'you have ever played so badly for so long a period?' There is no record of Jones's response. With his unfailing instinct for good manners, he wrote later that 'to agree would very obviously imply a disparagement of the opposition'. But it was the truth: 'By the hardest possible kind of labour I had managed to win these two tournaments when my game was never once anywhere near peak efficiency.'

This story by itself disposes of the natural assumption that Jones was on one of those hot streaks that happen once in a while to every golfer. His achievement was to have won his way through twenty-six rounds of golf (eleven at match play) over four summer months, punctuated by many distractions, including a trip to Paris, a transatlantic crossing, a Broadway ticker-tape parade and its attendant public ceremonies, not to mention two miraculous escapes from sudden death, one from a lightning bolt, the other from a runaway automobile. During the month between the two Opens he had time for only three practice rounds.

But even as Cyril Tolley put his rude questions, Jones's morale, the inner confidence that he could win the remaining two majors, had been greatly enhanced by the knowledge that he had come through what he later variously described as 'the most gruelling ordeal' of his career and 'the most important tournament of my life'. It was the British Amateur, the first of the four and the one in which Jones played his worst golf. Only in the eleventh(!) – the final – round, against Roger Wethered 'had things gone smoothly. One day it would be the long game, another the putting [and then] excellent play nullified by incredible lapses in concentration.'

But it was the final round, it now appears, that disclosed the secret (if it is one) of Jones's triumph. By a fluky twist of fate, it was against the giant Tolley and played at St Andrews in a thirty-mile-an-hour gale with 'the wind being whipped in the bunkers'. It was, in retrospect, the most decisive round of his life. 'Every victory,' he once wrote, 'has its element of luck.' And in the whole roster of twenty-six rounds, this was the one in which Jones enjoyed a stroke – two strokes, in fact – of luck at the most critical time. He was the first to point to it.

Dizzy with exhaustion and tied after eighteen holes, the two men padded back to the eighteenth tee and both hit long drives. Now came Tolley's fateful lapse. A 'slack second' (Jones's term) was followed by a weak chip, which left him lying three, seven feet from the hole. Jones, on pretty much the same line, was at ten feet in two. That gap of three feet was Fate's present to Jones and made possible the match, the Grand Slam, the ticker-tape parades and his subsequent unique fame. Jones putted up just two inches from the hole, precisely in Tolley's line. The big man conceded, and it was all over. Jones always regretted that 'such a splendid match' should have ended in a stymie;* but the stymie was in those days a challenging element

* The stymie was an integral though sometimes controversial part of match play until it was abolished in 1951. If an opponent's ball on the green was blocking your path to the hole, you were said to be 'stymied'. You were then faced with either playing round your opponent's ball or, if you had the skill, chipping over it. A stymie did not apply if the balls were less than six inches apart, and many old scorecards were deliberately made to that width in order to provide a handy ruler.

of play. (Understandably, Jones believed till the day he died that it should never have been abolished.)

Along the way of our search for the buried secret, Jones dropped a couple of markers. In an early column, he noticed and lamented the tendency of American golfers to go for 'length at the expense of accuracy and reliability'.

Thirty years later, he remarked that since the introduction of the steel shaft (to say nothing of the pitching wedge and Gene Sarazen's sand wedge) there was no longer any need to practise the four shots that 'must be mastered' to have a reliable short game: the short and long pitch, the run-up shot, the bump and run, and the chip, 'which can be anything from a 3-iron to a 9-iron'; all of which, he ruefully added, 'used to have to be played with one club and three variations of method and are now [in the 1960s] played with three clubs and no variations'. This gave the player (who had done the mastering) a wider choice of shots but also, in uncertain moments, a wider choice of errors. There is no question that before the fearsome torque of a hickory shaft became a mere memory, golf was a more difficult game to play – 'to play simply', as an old Scots caddie, who carried for Jones, used to say.

In the one piece that finally tells the tale of the Grand Slam feat, Jones reassures every hacker that even the finest players can at any time 'suddenly lose the feel', for the blunt reason that 'the human body was not constructed to accomplish a correct swing naturally'. (Elsewhere, he says it's the reason why no one will ever master the game of golf!) Now follows the single sentence in which he discovers and defines the discipline that helped him maintain what Bernard Darwin (reporting the last round of the British Amateur at St Andrews) called that rhythmic and unbroken stride through thirty-six holes. Jones's commenting sentence is the key. 'The golfer has always to be under restraint ... [like] that under which a trotting or pacing horse must labour to hold an artificial gait although his every urge is to run like blazes.'

What this meant to Jones, as a championship contestant

playing indifferently, was the unflagging exercise of a form of self-control excruciatingly more difficult than the well-worn injunction to 'keep your cool'. In the light of these reflections, we can now see that more than the reward of skill or luck, the Grand Slam was a feat of character.

7

The Written Record

1980

Every sport pretends to a literature, but people don't believe it of any sport but their own. Ask Herbert Warren Wind or Ben Crenshaw to guess who is writing about what in the following passage, and he might cite Horace Hutchinson writing in 1903 on the never-ending problem of the swing: 'The art, though difficult, may be acquired by imitation of a good practitioner, and, once it is mastered, constitutes one of those delightful combinations of strength and delicacy in which is found the chief charm of the higher athletics.' The real author, however, had probably never heard of the golf swing, though he is or was – I am told – the revered master of the grilse, the gilaroo, the finnock, the sewin and every other guise of salmon. He is Sir Herbert Maxwell talking about the art of 'casting the fly'. Indeed, as I was settling to write the piece, my doctor was dangling before me the improbable dream of a million-dollar market for an anthology of fishing literature. All I could think of was Izaak Walton, Hemingway, and Red Smith* (for that matter, Red Smith can create a literature of any sport he cares to write about). But, the doc insists, there is an enormous literature of fishing. I take his word for it and leave him to it.

I know there is a cricket literature, beginning – as far as I'm concerned (which is not very far) – with 'a breathless hush in the Close tonight' and ending with Neville Cardus. And for

---

* Walter Wellesley 'Red' Smith (1905–1982): American journalist who became America's most widely read sportswriter while working on the *New York Herald Tribune* and then the *New York Times*.

the sake of peace at any price, we had better assume that there is an impressive literature also of curling, gin rummy and table tennis. But, now, golf. Does anybody – except the entire world of non-golfers – deny that 'the gowf' has produced the richest literature of any known sport?

Granted that to get any pleasure from golf reporting (i.e., 'fired a 3-iron to the tenth ... sank a fifteen-footer at the twelfth ... fashioned four birdies, two bogeys and two long par-saving putts for a third-round 68') it helps to know the difference between a 3-iron and a branding iron; although it is debatable whether, since the invention of the transistorised edit terminal, any pleasure at all is to be had from news-agency reporting. But this daily drone bears about as much relationship to the literature of golf as the stock market index does to the romance of money, as revealed in, say, a biography of J. P. Morgan or the novels of Balzac. Every Sunday for forty years, the late lamented Henry Longhurst kept a devoted following, at least thirty per cent of whom had never lifted a golf club or were likely to. He saw golf as an ample outdoor stage on which a cast of Dickensian characters was compelled by the firm etiquette of the game to act out a script by Jane Austen. The unique, the furtive pleasure that golf offers to the inveterate spectator – whether on the ground or on the box – is something that is not required of the ecstatic goal scorer or the tennis player in a tantrum: the tension of restraint. Once in a while, Johnny Miller may groan at the skies, Trevino may bark at his ball as at an errant puppy. But in moments of crushing disappointment, not even Sam Snead and Tom Weiskopf browbeat a marshal: they explode in a sigh. One great opportunity of tournament report-ing, variously seized by such as Dan Jenkins, Bernard Darwin and Michael Williams, is to sense the turmoil or the ruefulness going on inside the placid exterior of a possible winner two strokes back with five holes to play. In short, character, and the tracing of its foibles, is only one of the things that the game is about. It has been enough to make memorable the entire golfing output of P. G. Wodehouse, Stephen Leacock, and Jim Murray.

But the game is complex enough, and beautiful and leisurely enough, to open up all sorts of specialties for all sorts of writers. Unlike, shall we say, tennis or chess, golf has an incomparable range of landscape, which encourages Pat Ward-Thomas to delineate the different pains and pleasures of the chase in Scotland and France and the California desert; John Updike to peel off the social layers from the artichoke of Augusta, Georgia; and Charles Price to enlarge on his lifelong feud with practically any course that gets the better of him.

There is the fantasy, indulged by every hacker on his pillow, of playing with Nicklaus or Palmer – and George Plimpton* actually did it and put the experience into humiliating prose.

There is even – as with no other game – a fascinating detective literature, a wry commentary on the human comedy, implicit in the book of rules. I must say that for a game whose aim is to get a little ball in a hole in as few strokes as possible, the book of rules would seem to offer, at first glance, less excitement than the propositions of Euclid. In fact, and precisely because golf is played on a board of 120 acres or more, the vagaries of weather and topography, not to mention the unpredictable whimsies and prejudices of the human animal at play, have produced shelves of legal commentaries on the rules that suggest to the imaginative reader as many subtle and hilarious interpretations as the Constitution of the United States. Anyone who doubts this should run, not walk, to procure the entertaining gloss on the rules recently written by Frank Hannigan with Tom Watson standing watchfully at his elbow.

I suppose that the least satisfactory prose in the whole body of the literature (it is also true of the literature of any other game) is that devoted to describing the technique of how it is done or ought to be done. This is a nearly inevitable failing, since God decreed that the doers of this world are seldom, if ever, writers. Nobody has yet written a *Sudden Death in the Afternoon* to

* George Plimpton (1927–2003): American journalist, writer, editor, and actor. Author of many books on different sports including *The Bogey Man* about his experiences travelling with the PGA Tour.

compare with Hemingway's bone-clear exposition of how a bull is fought. But pending this masterpiece, several famous players and their ghosts have made a brave stab at it. And the great one who never needed a ghost, Robert Tyre Jones, has left us an incomparable file of lucid and literate commentaries.

8

Pottermanship*

1968

To say that this book (*The Complete Golf Gamesmanship* by Stephen Potter) is a landmark study in human sensibility comparable to the Old Testament or Freud's *Interpretation of Dreams* is, of course, obvious. But it is not yet obvious to the Establishment, whose members are uncomfortable with Potter's insights and tend to gather in corners and mumble about 'sportsmanship'. But no one has demonstrated better than Potter that sportsmanship is death to the spirit of gamesmanship. Sportsmanship produces nothing but decent, kindly, fair-minded, *petits bourgeois*.

The fact is that until Potter, laying aside his former pre-occupations with D. H. Lawrence and Samuel Taylor Coleridge, published his pioneer work, *Gamesmanship*, so long ago as 1947, our knowledge of human hypocrisy and how it might be exploited for the well-being of the exploiter was haphazard at best. Dickens had done some rough experimental work in his – what is it? – fifteen novels. Alexander Pope was no slouch at celebrating the rich meanness of the human spirit. Machiavelli, of course, was the true forerunner of Potter, but his insights, and the technique of deception we can develop from them, were never systematised. It was left to Potter to throw a great light, in three modest monographs, on the wonderful possibilities of cheating under the guise of loving thy neighbour. It is Potter, not

* A review of *The Complete Golf Gamesmanship*, by Stephen Potter, Heinemann, London, 1968.

44

Freud or McLuhan or Marcuse, not Bertrand Russell or Isaiah Berlin, or any such simpleton, who has truly discovered the tough, tart root of human behaviour – *like it is* – and who, in his new book, shows us in no more than 177 cogent pages, the way to a fuller, more deceitful life.

Even the index to this book is a revelation. Other men's indexes, or indices, are stark guideposts to a sprawling terrain of births, marriages, deaths and other, if any, mortal statistics. Potter's index shows the range of his mastery of the continuing war between man and woman, man and man, pro and amateur, brother and brother-in-law, snob and counter-snob. For example: 'Cuffey, made to feel poor, 52'; 'Cornpetter, Major, fails to snub Tickler, 32'; 'Anti-anti-Semite play, 144'; 'Darwin, W. R., his indifference to innocent pride ploy, 74'; 'Woking, route to, how to argue about, 34'; 'Valjean, Jean, misplaced remorse of, 160'; 'United States, clubhouse comforts of, how to counter, 103'.

It will be fussily argued by some readers that Potter is writing about golf. Nothing could be further from the truth. You might as well say that in *Othello* Shakespeare was writing about a handkerchief. Potter simply uses golf as his locale in which to tap the secret springs in all of us – well, in some of us – of Simon Legreemanship, Mata Harimanship, Lyndon Baines Johnsonmanship. If this were a mere history of golf, you would expect to read a great deal about Robert Tyre (Bobby) Jones, the greatest golfer of his time, some say of any time. But here, in Potter, there is only one brief, regretful paragraph about him, for the simple reason that Jones was a sportsman, in the anachronistic sense our grandfathers used: a genuinely good man. 'Many heads are shaken,' writes Potter 'when his name comes up.'

Potter chose golf, above all other games, through which to expound about life because (he once wrote when he was under the influence of James Joyce) 'it is the game of games' for employing the human resources of pretence: pretended admiration, pretended courage, pretended hurt, stoicism, indifference and so on and on. He makes clear at the start that his prime concern is with life, for as he says, in brilliantly demolishing the oldest cliché, 'it is not golf that is a microcosm of life, but rather that life is golf in miniature'.

He begins with a penetrating history of the game that will replace once and for all the tedious chronicles that plod through all the boring progressions of the game from the feathery to the rubber-cored, from Holland to Scotland to South Carolina to Yonkers. His starting point is the usefulness of idiosyncrasy (bordering on hypocrisy) in the Scottish character, moves on to the growth of the Englishman's gift for exploiting 'one down-manship', and winds up with a brilliant and persuasive explanation of how the United States came to dominate the game in the 1920s. Like all great historical truths, it is very simple, and it is best expressed through the actions of one Great Man. The American conquest was due, we learn, to the appearance in Britain of 'the King Gamesman', Walter Hagen, and had little to do with 'his thread of skill'. He was the first American actually to intimidate the most confident Britons. He systematically overtipped his caddie. He hired a Rolls to take him to the *side door* of the clubs he was to play at (since, as a professional, he was not allowed in the main rooms). His great achievement, however, was to introduce and flaunt the two-tone shoe – soon to be known from Brighton to Cannes as the 'co-respondent's shoe'. He thus blithely transferred to the British his own inferiority complex, from which they have never recovered.

For precocious students of Potter there is the joy of discovering that the Master has greatly enlarged and developed his pioneering work. Here the diligent student of the ploy and counter ploy may go on to practise the Secondary Hamper, the Pour, the Baltusrol and many another device for reducing one's partner (opponent?) in life, in golf, in business, in marriage, to dithering acquiescence or even frank surrender. It is a happy thing that the book appears at Christmas. Potter can be recommended whole-heartedly to those who prefer to believe that the Christian era is over, and that henceforth it is the bland and the sly who shall inherit the earth.

9

Walter Hagen 1892–1969

1969

Every golfer who has read the books or listened to the Oldest Member knows about Hagen's iron play, his incredible recoveries, the thrust of his right shoulder to the target, his dependable quota of atrocious shots, and how he arrived in Britain to win the Open and wound up fifty-fifth. But to recapture his stunning effect on Britain and British golf, you have paradoxically to forget about golf and see him strutting into the social scene of the 1920s. For – to the query of the young, 'What was so great about Hagen?' – the only possible answer is: his character, which was achieved without benefit of public relations releases or image-makers.

When Hagen arrived at Deal in 1920, there were no 'talkies' or television news roundups. And throughout the Twenties, few Englishmen knew even what an American sounded like. He was a species of exotic. All the ordinary Englishman had to go on, unless he had billeted some doughboys in the First War, was Woodrow Wilson preaching soundless sermons in the newsreels and Gertrude Ederle, the Channel swimmer, grinning at ecstatic little men in bowlers as she sloshed ashore at Dover. Most of us in those days kept a file at the back of our minds of what we took to be the standard American types, compiled naturally from the silent movies. Wallace Reid was the clean-cut, sensitive young man, Warner Oland was an early prototype of the Mafia, William S. Hart was every rancher west of the Mississippi, Lew Cody was the boudoir villain, and Douglas Fairbanks was – Douglas Fairbanks.

So, who was this Hagen, with the head of a seal, the sleepy eyes, the peacock sweaters and co-respondent's shoes, and his much-publicised love of the high life? He looked like the 'lounge lizard' all nice girls were warned against. He looked like a young associate of Warner Oland out after Pearl White's inheritance. The outrageous anecdotes supported this suspicion: a mere pro hiring a chauffeur and a champagne lunch, whamming golf balls into the Thames from the Savoy roof, calling the Prince of Wales 'David', indeed! Today we chuckle, but in the beginning the chuckles were punctuated by pained cries from the Old Guard whom the Lord sent Hagen to mock. His original, and imperishable, appeal was that he confounded all our preconceptions about the 'typical' American. He was a walking contradiction, a preposterous and engaging amalgam of types that were supposed to be poles apart. He could battle a golf course like Fairbanks, mutter snide remarks like W. C. Fields, and be as chivalrous as Bobby Jones. He was Lew Cody and Fairbanks and Wallace Reid all in one. And small boys like me, cricketing maniacs who had no interest in golf as such, dived on summer mornings for Tom Webster's cartoons of him to revel in what my father called 'a card and no mistake'.

There was a time in and around New York and Hollywood when almost any famous witty line was attributed to Dorothy Parker. Hagen had a similar gift for annexing any hilarious, anti-Establishment anecdote and making it his own. 'Who's going to be second?' 'Your opponent's been in bed for two hours.' 'He may be in bed but he's not asleep.' 'Hold the flag, David!' These are tag lines as familiar to golfers as 'Never ... was so much owed by so many to so few' and 'Some chicken, some neck' are familiar to every free man who remembers how much of his freedom he owes to Winston Churchill.

When other great players will be remembered only by the photographs of their swing and the tournament statistics, Walter Hagen will be immortal for certain other records that recall not so much his prowess as his brash charm and his delight in the game: the first man to give his caddie all the prize money; the first, and perhaps the only, first-class player who had the gall to have the flag removed for a long-iron approach from about 170 yards; the only professional who ever jerked a putt out of bounds; and always the only golfer who honestly and always forgot the last bad hole. For these things and also for the remark, practically a capsule philosophy, that does not dim by endless repetition and which would have made the perfect epitaph for his gravestone: 'Take time to smell the flowers.'

10

Make Way for the Senior Golfer

1971

Do you want to hear about my 39 on the tough back nine at Noyac, a fairly new – but, as we oldsters like to say, a 'testing' – course at the end of Long Island? Well, you're going to.

I will make the account of this masterful round brief, but only out of consideration for those lobster-tanned veterans who took up the game at the age of eight, progressed by kangaroo stages to a 2 handicap and have deteriorated so alarmingly with each decade that when asked to exercise total recall and recount the history of some of their triumphs they reply, like Bing Crosby, 'Total recall? I can't even recall when I last broke 80.'

Well, sir, it was a glittering Sunday afternoon in the late fall. I was sitting out on our terrace on the North Fork of Long Island facing the deep blue waters of Peconic Bay and feeling pretty hot under the collar. We had had three people to lunch. We were still having them to lunch and it was twenty-five minutes to four, a whole hour past the time when I normally have bussed my wife with resounding gratitude, torn off to a links course twelve miles away and started to lace long drives and cunning little pitches – alone, of course – into the declining sun. I had already given rather gross notice to these dawdlers of my intentions by retreating to my bedroom and going through my normal medical routine as a senior golfer (we shall come to that a little later on).

Our guests – my lawyer, his wife and sister – would have been, at any other time, enchanting company. In fact, until they started on their third lobster at 3.00 p.m. I was convinced that no more amiable guests had ever wolfed our vodka or darkened our towels.

Far off, across the old Colonial meadows at our back, a church clock struck three-thirty. The old Colonial churches still have their uses, not the least of which is to toll the knell of parting guests. My lawyer turned to me and said: 'A beautiful time of day, this, especially in the fall.' In a flash, I saw my opportunity for a cliff-hanger's cry. 'Yes, indeed,' I said, 'you know, a friend of mine now pattering towards the grave told me that when he gets to Heaven – he is what they always call a *devout* Catholic and he has no anxiety whatsoever about his destination – and is asked by St Peter what, if he had lived longer, he would most wish to have prolonged, he will reply – "late afternoon golf".'

'That's right,' said my lawyer, 'you usually play around this time, don't you?'

I furtively leaned over to him while the ladies were still slurping up the repulsive butter and lemon sauce. '*Around* this time,' I said with a meaningful ogle. '*By* this time I am usually recording my first par on the very difficult fourth hole whose green recedes invisibly into Long Island Sound.'

He is a guileless man – except in all matters pertaining to residuals and cassette rights – and he started as a fox might start out of its burrow on our fast-eroding bank or bluff. 'Listen,' he whispered beseechingly, 'don't let us stop you ...'

I stopped him right there and begged the ladies to round things off with a liqueur. 'A dram of cognac, a *soupçon* of kirsch?' I suggested. 'Goodness, no thanks,' – thank goodness – they said.

'Really,' he implored.

'I tell you what,' I said, now in complete control of a situation not even imagined by the late, great Stephen Potter, 'we are going to dinner on the South Shore not far from you. Why doesn't Jane drive your ladies over an hour or so from now, *when they are ready to leave*? You and I will take your car, whisk around a fast eighteen holes at Island's End, and then we'll meet them all back at your place?'

I anticipated his next line, which was, 'You know, I'm ashamed to say I don't play, but I love to walk around. D'you think I could just amble along?'

The trajectory of our departure was never matched by Bugs Bunny. Fifteen seconds later we were on our way, leaving the women to surmise, 'Did they go for a swim? Irving doesn't really care for swimming.'

Island's End is a semi-public course, which means that at unpredictable times it is likely to be infested by a couple of busloads of the Associated Potato and Cauliflower Growers of Long Island. It was such a day. 'No way,' said the young pro, 'there are seventy-five of them out there and you wouldn't get through five holes before dark.'

'Too bad,' said my honest lawyer.

'I retain,' I said, 'an escape clause for just such emergencies. I am a member at Noyac on the South Shore, and on Sundays not even guests can play.'

We snorted off to the ferry, trundled across the Bay, roared the five miles to the North Haven ferry, made it, and thundered up to the pro shop at Noyac on the stroke of five. To all such jocularities as 'trying out a little bit of night golf, eh, Mr Cooke?' I turned a contemptuous ear. We were in an electric cart in one minute flat. (I hasten to say to snobs from the Surrey pine-and-sand country that no invention since the corn plaster or the electric toothbrush has brought greater balm to the extremities of the senior golfer than the golfmobile, a word that will have to do for want of a better.)

A natural and chronic modesty forbids my taking you stroke by flawless stroke through the following nine holes. ('I think we'll take the back nine,' I had muttered to my lawyer, 'it's a little more testing.') Suffice it to say that when we approached the dreaded eleventh – an interminable par 5 with a blind second shot up to a plateau three yards wide between two Grand Canyon bunkers – my friend was already goggling in the car or cart stammering out such memorable asides as, 'I don't believe it, it looks so goddamn easy.'

An imperious drive had put me in the prescribed position for the perilous second shot. I was lining myself up, with the image of Nicklaus very vivid in my mind, when I noticed two large gorillas disturbing my peripheral vision. I paused and looked up in total, shivering control. Happily, on closer inspection, they turned out not to be gorillas but two typical young American golfers in their late twenties. They were about six feet three each, they carried the dark give-away tan that betokens the 4-handicapper, and they waved at me nonchalantly and said, 'Go ahead, grandpa, we've got all the time in the world.'

Again I went through my casual Nicklaus motions. My 3-wood followed the absolutely necessary arc and the ball came to rest precisely midway between the two bunkers.

'Many thanks,' I said briskly and waved back at the aghast gorillas. They marched fifty yards or so to what I was crestfallen to realise were their drives. Gallantly I indicated that no matter what the humiliation to me they should proceed. They banged two stout shots, one into the right bunker, the other on the edge of the pine woods.

By the time I came up to my ball, I was sitting upright with a commanding expression worthy of Adolf Hitler arriving in Vienna in his hand-made Opel. The gorillas paused again, and waved again. 'Go ahead,' they said.

''Enks vemmuch,' I said. I took a 5-iron with all the slow calculation of Geronimo Hogan. Ahead lay a great swale, another swirl of bunkers, a plateau and the bunkers guarding the sloping green. I heard in my ears the only sentence I have ever heard at the moment of address from George Heron, my old Scottish teacher of seventy-eight summers, springs and winters: 'Slow along the ground, big turn, hit out to me.'

It rose slowly like a gull sensing a reckless bluefish too close to the surface, and then it dived relentlessly for the green, kicked and stopped three feet short of the flag.

'Jesus!' cried one of the gorillas, 'd'you hit the ball this way all the time?'

'Not,' I replied, 'since I left the tour.'

We left them gasping. And to be truthful, I left the ninth hole gasping.

'You never told me!' shouted my beloved friend and lawyer.

'I never knew,' I said.

It was the kind of round that I play every night on the pillow but never, at any other time, on a golf course. As the man said, 'It looks so goddamn easy.'

Every golfer who reads these historic words has played such a round. But few know the secret of a senior golfer's total relaxation. I am about to confide it to you. While other men change their slacks, down a Scotch and head for the first tee, the really thoughtful senior golfer knows that before he leaves his house he must follow a routine that will take a decade off his life and give him the illusion of careless youth.

First, then, the toenails in old age grow almost as fast as the ears and the nose. There is nothing you can do about them but you can spend a minute or two trimming the toenails. Next, swallow a couple of Bufferin against the old back injury. Next, a swift application of some mild anaesthetic for the bothersome scar tissue from that old haemorrhoidectomy. Don't forget the Tums, Bisodol or simply a packet of sodium bicarbonate as a precaution against indigestion. Clean the spectacles. Rub a little resin on the last three fingers of the left hand. Stand up straight – think of Raquel Welch. (On second thoughts, don't think of Raquel Welch.) Comb the hair smoothly and think of the swing of Dave Marr. Walk very slowly, masterfully, to the first tee. Put on the cap bought in Edinburgh and think of Hogan. Stand up straight.

That is all. Cypress? Pebble Beach? Pine Valley? The Old Course, anyone?

II

A Perfect Day for Golf

1968

At the end of the first day of last year's [US] Open [at Baltusrol] when the temperature inside the press tent was, as I recall, 110 and a black sky was coming up like the Day of Judgment, the old veterans of these campaigns swabbed up the rivers of sweat that were blurring their immortal prose and wondered when the USGA would pick, once for all, the right place at the right time to hold a comfortable Open. They began to call off the famous occasions when plump heroes had teed off at noon and staggered in like wraiths in the evening, with or without doctors in attendance: Craig Wood at Fort Worth in 1941, Hogan beaten down by his own Texas sun at Dallas in 1952, Dick Mayer at Toledo in '57, Venturi at Washington in '64. No one not suffering from gross astigmatism could ever have called Nicklaus a wraith at any time of his life, but at Baltusrol last year even he set a new record in the cola consumption singles (twelve bottles on the last round).

Tom Flaherty's history of the Open is peppered with phrases that sound like quotes from Milton's *Paradise Lost*: 'the old warrior worn out by heat', 'dripping wet from head to shoe', 'rain and lightning broke the ninety-five degrees', 'And not the sweating multitudes.'

At this point, Frank Hannigan* came by to defend the Establishment. He was clanking with walkie-talkies and wrapped in

---

* Frank Hannigan (b. 1931): former USGA executive director; now an ABC Sports commentator.

telephone wires and looked like a certified public accountant in a space movie. He could prove, by simply pressing buttons, that the Open has been held too in the stratosphere of Denver, the tundra of Minneapolis, and twice in the cool paradise of San Francisco. But most of the sixty-eight contests held so far have been sweated out in the inferno of the continental mainland. At the mention of the Golden Gate, a veil of tears glazed the hot eyeballs of the oldest member present. 'Ah,' he said, 'if only they'd hold it every year at Olympic or San Francisco or Pebble Beach.'

This brings up the great underground debate which goes on, I have noticed, unceasingly among golfers who ever travel much; but which never seems to burst into print. It is the question of the ideal place and weather in which to play the beautiful, damnable game. My researches have taken me from St Andrews through Africa and Asia and back again, and I can only say that it seems to be a matter as personal as your definition of the bearable night-time temperature of a bedroom. I have always lamented that the progressive schools – and now, Heaven help us, the seminarians – befog their pupils with gobs of sex education but never offer instruction in the only thing that can really break or make a marriage, for before a man marries it should be compulsory for him to find out whether he is going to be bedded down for the rest of his life with a polar bear or a coolie.

The Texans to a man maintain that 85 (on a golf course, that is) is just right, and they tend to snivel and whine when they are required to move north of the Pecos River. The Scots, at the other pole – so to speak – regard a damp 42, with the offshore winds whistling up a storm, as the only proper test of the game. I met an old man in Glasgow last year who boasted that he had long abided by three rules. He would never play in a temperature over 60 degrees (63 is normal August high in Glasgow), on a course that contained a tree or on a day when there was little wind. 'Othairwise,' he laid down, 'ye're no playin' goff.' On the other hand, there was an Englishman in Bangkok, the local champion of the diplomatic corps, who regretted that he had been called back to home duty. He would miss, he said, 'the good sweat' (Bangkok is worse even than Baltusrol).

In Rochester, Minnesota, they boast (how correctly I do not know) that they have more golf courses within, or just without, the city limits than any other city in the United States. They forget to add that they are unplayable, by most visitors from the temperate zone, except in the summer – late June to mid-August. In Hawaii, they maintain they have the best all-year-round golf weather on the globe, the assumption being that the game cannot be played at under 80 degrees Fahrenheit. The Scots assume that wind is as necessary a hazard as a bunker. From the Carolinas south they put two sweaters on if the mercury goes below 70. In old York they like to say they can play all year, and so you can if you regard 45 degrees and a knifing, wet east wind as essential to health. But in New York, I know people who won't go out except on dead still days in the 60s with no clouds in sight. Myself, I look on January, February and March as the blackest months of the year.

The golf commentators in their writings always imply but never say out loud exactly what is the perfect place and the 'perfect day' for golf. Would it not be simple for Joe Dey to poll the entire professional roster, strike a favourite moan, and pick on the agreed time and place? It would be simpler still, of course, to settle for the same time and place every year: San Francisco in June, July, August, September or October.

12

Snow, Cholera, Lions, and Other Distractions

1975

Just after dawn on a brisk but brilliant December day a couple of years ago, I was about to ask Raquel Welch if she was all set for a droll caper I had in mind, when the telephone went off like a fire alarm, and an eager voice shouted, 'All set?' It was, alas, not Raquel but my golf partner, a merry banker of indestructible cheerfulness who calls all stock-market recessions 'healthy shakeouts'. I climbed out of my promising dream and out of bed, and in no time I was washing the irons, downing the Bufferin, rubbing resin on the last three fingers of the left hand, inserting the plastic heel cup, searching for my Hogan cap – performing the whole early morning routine of the senior golfer. This was the great day we had promised ourselves ever since I had suffered the shock of hearing Herbert Warren Wind confess he had never played Century, the tough and beautiful rolling course in Purchase, New York, where Ben Hogan had his first job as a teaching pro. It seemed ridiculous that the man who had helped Hogan lay down *The Fundamentals of Modern Golf* should never have played the course on which Ben laid them down. Another telephone call alerted Wind to get the hell out of his variation on the Welch fantasy. An hour later we were on our way, up the West Side Highway and the Saw Mill River Parkway, and on to Purchase.

Century is the private domain of some very well-heeled gents from Wall Street, but they are so busy watching those healthy shakeouts that none of them has much time for weekday golf. Furthermore, in December, the caviar and hamburgers are stacked in the deep freeze. But, since it is very difficult to close a golf course, the course is open. The caddie master had been briefed about the signal honour that Wind was going to confer on one of the fifty toughest courses in America and he had obligingly mobilised two of his veteran caddies.

As we swung around White Plains and began to thread up through the country lanes of Purchase, we were puzzled to see strips of white cement smearing the grassy banks of the highway. They got thicker as we turned into the club driveway, and as we came out on the hill that overlooks the undulating terrain, we saw that the whole course was overlaid not with cement but with snow. The caddies were already there and looking pretty glum. They greeted us by stomping their feet and slapping their ears and otherwise conveying that, though our original idea was a brave one, it had obviously been aborted by the weather. 'You serious about this thing, Mr Manheim?' one of the caddies asked the banker. 'Sure,' said Manheim, who would play golf in a hammock if that's what the rules called for.

We started off with three reasonable drives, which scudded into the snow the way Hawaiian surfers skim under a tidal wave. The caddies went after them like ferrets and, after a lot of burrowing and signalling, retrieved them and stood there holding the balls and looking at us, as the song says, square down in the eye, as if to say, 'What are you going to do with these damn things?' We had to find little slivers of exposed ground (no nearer the hole) and drop them and swipe off once more. The greens were either iced over or had sheets of ice floating in little lakes. After several five-putts on the first two greens, we decided that anybody who could hold a green deserved the concession of two putts.

This went on for eight holes, at the end of which, however, Wind allowed that Hogan sure loved to set himself problems. Plodding up the long ninth fairway, with Cooke beginning to turn blue and the banker humming happily to himself (it was the two-putt rule that did it), Wind turned and said, 'Tell me, Manheim, do you do this because you're nuts or because your

PR man says it's good for your image?' We three-putted the ninth green, which 'held' with the consistency of rice pudding, and that was it.

As I recall this Arctic expedition, there is a blustery wind bending the trees in Central Park and a steady rain, a combination of circumstances that fires many a Scotsman to rush out and play a round of golf in what one of them once told me are 'the only propair condeetions'. But, because this is America, they are conditions that immediately empty the golf courses from Maine to San Diego, forcing the sons of the pioneers to clean their clubs, putt on the bedroom carpet or sink into the torpor of watching a football game. We have it from the Mexican ambassador himself, His Excellency Lee Trevino, that there are Texans who will not play at all whenever the temperature toboggans below 80 degrees Fahrenheit. And there are by now many generations of Dutchmen who gave up the game once it moved off ice on to grass.

It is a wonderful tribute to the game or to the dottiness of the people who play it that for some people somewhere there is no such thing as an insurmountable obstacle, an unplayable course, the wrong time of the day or the year. Last year I took Manheim – whose idea of a beautiful golf course is a beautiful park – to play his first links course. It is the home course of the English golf writer Pat Ward-Thomas. (Ward-Thomas's idea of the most beautiful golf course in the world is his home course.) It is up in the bleak stretch of south-eastern England known as Norfolk, a sort of miniature prairie exposed to the winds whistling out of Siberia. The course is called Brancaster, and you can drive up to the rude clubhouse, a kind of Charles Addams gabled shack, and start asking people where is the golf course. For ahead of you is nothing but flat marshland – which floods at the high tide – and beyond that the grey North Sea and a chorus of squawking gulls. The flags are about two feet high, so as to encourage the notion that man has not been known to tamper with a masterpiece of nature.

When we went into lunch it was spitting rain and when we

came out it was raining stair rods. The wind gauge at the club-house entrance registered 43 knots. There was Ward-Thomas; a handsome and imperturbable Englishman named Tom Harvey; Manheim and I. There were also two caddies, aged about ten, already half-drowned and cowering in the whirling sand like two fugitives from Dotheboys Hall.

Nobody raised a question or lifted an eyebrow, so Manheim and I – remembering the good old White House slogan – soldiered on. By about the seventh, Manheim, who wears glasses, had to be guided to the proper tees. We were all so swollen with sweaters and raingear we looked like the man in the Michelin ads. Well, sir, they talked throughout in well-modulated tones about 'sharp doglegs' and 'a rather long carry' and 'it's normally an easy 5-iron, but maybe with this touch of wind you'd be safer with a 4-iron, even a 4-wood, I shouldn't wonder.' We were now all waterlogged, from the toenails to the scalp, and Manheim came squelching over to me and said, 'Are these guys nuts?' I told him that on the contrary this was for them a regular outing: 'You know what the Scotsman said – "If there's nae wind, it's nae gawf."' Manheim shook his head like a drenched terrier and plodded on. The awful thing was that Harvey, a pretty formidable golfer, was drawing and fading the damn thing at will, this proving the sad truth that if you hit it right, even a tornado is not much of a factor.

Outward bound, we'd been carried downwind. But as we were bouncing like tumbleweed down to the ninth green, Ward-Thomas came staggering over. I should tell you that he is a gaunt and a very engaging gent and he has a vocabulary that would have qualified him for an absolutely top advisory post in the last Republican administration. He came at me with his spiky hair plastered against his forehead and water bobbing off his nose and chin. He screamed confidentially into the gale: 'If you think this (expletive deleted) nine is a (expletive deleted) picnic, wait till we come to the (expletive deleted) turn!'

He was right. We could just about stand in the teeth of the gale, but the balls kept toppling off the tees. It was a time to make you yearn for the old sandbox.* Manheim's glasses now looked like the flooded windshield of a gangster escaping through a hurricane in an old Warner Brothers movie. Moreover, his tweed hat kept swivelling around, making him stand to the ball like a guy who'd been taught about his master eye by a one-eyed pirate. At this point, Ward-Thomas offered up the supreme sacrifice. He is a long-time idolater of Arnold Palmer and he cried, 'Hold it!' and plunged into his bag. He came up with a faded sun hat and tendered it to Manheim with the reverent remark: 'It was given to me by Palmer. Try it.' As everybody knows, Palmer's head is on the same scale as his forearms, and this one blotted out Manheim's forehead, nose, glasses, master eye and all. What we did from then on was to slop our way down the last nine, pity the trembling caddies and throw murderous glances at Harvey, who was firing beautiful woods into the hurricane.

Very little was said as we retired to Harvey's home, fed every strip of clothing into a basement stove and stewed in baths that would have scalded a Turk. At dinner it came out. All through the first nine, Harvey and Ward-Thomas had been muttering to each other just as Manheim and I had been doing: 'They must be out of their minds, but if this is what they're used to . . .' Harvey said, 'We decided that since you were our guests, the only thing to do was to stick it out.'

If these are fair samples of maniacal golfers, how about crazy golf courses?

You would not think, looking at the stony rampart of the mountain face behind Monte Carlo, that anyone could plant a one-hole putting green between those slabs of granite. But when you get to the top, there the indomitable British have somehow contrived a course that lurches all around the Maritime Alps. There is rarely a straightaway drive. On the very first tee, you jump up in the air and see the flag fluttering in a depression way

---

* In golf's earlier days, before wooden or plastic tee-pegs became the norm, the ball was rested on a small quantity of sand which was kept in a box beside each tee.

to the left. You ask the caddie for the line. He points with a Napoleonic gesture to a mountain far to the right. 'La ligne!' he commands. And if you believe him and bang away at the mountain-top, you then see the ball come toppling about a hundred yards to the left and going out of sight. Which is the proper trajectory to the green.

The golf 'clubu' at Istanbul is, if anything, more improbable still. The banks of the Bosporus are studded with more boulders than Vermont. But when the Scots took Constantinople at the end of World War I and laid in an adequate supply of their *vin du pays*, what else was there to do but build a golf course? The original rude layout is still there in the 'clubu' house, and on paper it looks like a golf course. In fact, it is simply a collection of flags stuck at random on a mountainside of boulders. Every ball comes to rest against a rock. The local rule is a free drop on every stroke. You drop it and drop it till it stops, and never mind the fussy business of 'no nearer the hole'.

In Bangkok, before the natives took to cement and the automobile, the canals looked like irrigation ditches slicing every fairway. Forecaddies,* as nimble as grasshoppers, spent the day diving into the canals and surfacing with an ear-to-ear grin while they held aloft a ball drenched with cholera. Once they'd wiped it and dropped it, you were on your way again, and free to enjoy the great game in a dripping temperature of 110 degrees.

A lion, you might guess, is not a normal item of wildlife on your course or mine. But in Nairobi once, a tawny monster strolled out of the woods, sniffed at my ball and padded off again, while my partner, a British native of the place, tweaked his moustache and drawled, 'You're away, I think.' At about the third hole I pushed my drive into the woods, and when I started

---

* A forecaddie was an additional caddie employed to show where a player's ball had landed or to indicate when a blind shot could be safely played. They have been banned in formal golf since the 1950s as it was felt that they gave players who could afford them an unfair advantage over their opponent. There is, however, nothing to stop competition organisers from providing 'spotters' to the benefit of all competitors.

after it, the host screamed at me to cease and desist. 'Snakes, man, snakes!' he hissed; 'leave it to the forecaddies.' They plunged into shoulder-high underbrush, and I meekly muttered, 'How about *them*?' 'Them?' the man said, 'Good God, they're marvellous. Splendid chaps; lost only two this year.' That round, I recall, was something of a nightmare, what with my pushed drives and the caddies (the ones who survived) chattering away in Swahili. The whole place was so exotic that I began to wonder if any of the normal rules of golf applied. One time, we came on a sign which read, 'GUR'. I gave it the full Swahili treatment. 'What,' I said, 'does GHOOOR mean?' He gave a slight start, as if some hippo were pounding in from the shade. Then he saw the sign. 'That,' he said firmly, 'means Ground Under Repair.' And he sighed and started to hum a Sousa march. After all, you must expect anything in golf. A stranger comes through; he's keen for a game; he seems affable enough, and on the eighth fairway he turns out to be an idiot. It's the rub of the green, isn't it?

Well, it takes more sorts than you and I have dreamed of to make up the world of golf. In Japan, they take a ski lift up to the tee of a famous par 3. In Cannes, the club members never bat an eyelid as they board a ferry from one green to the next tee.

But for sheer systematic nuttiness, nothing can compare with an annual ceremony put on by the Oxford and Cambridge Golfing Society, a collection of leather-elbowed oldsters and shaggy-haired youngsters who play for the President's Putter, no less, every year in the first week of January at Rye, on the coast of Sussex, another treeless links course fronting on a marsh which gives out into the English Channel. This tournament is intended to prove the English boast that 'we can play golf every day of the year'. If they can do it at Rye in January, they can do it at the South Pole, which in some sharp ways Rye resembles. At any rate, under the supervision of Gerald Micklem,* a peppery stockbroker in his sixties who is the Genghis Khan of British

* Gerald Micklem (1911–1988): British amateur golfer, played in the Walker Cup between 1947 and 1955, and captained the team in 1957 and 1959. Won the Amateur championship in 1947 and 1953.

amateur golf, these maniacs go through with this tournament on the scheduled date no matter what. Snow, hail, wind, torrents – nothing can keep them from the swift completion of their Micklem-appointed rounds.

I was there four years ago. On the first morning, the small town and the course were completely obliterated in a fog denser than anything in Dickens. It seeped into the hotels so you needed a links boy to light your way to your plate of bacon, baps and bangers. I assumed the whole thing was off, till a telephone call warned a few dallying competitors that their tee-off time was about to strike. We crawled out to the course, and the first person I ran into, marching around the clubhouse, was Micklem. I asked him if anyone was out there, and if so, why. 'Nonsense,' he barked. 'They're all out there. Haven't lost a ball yet.' He motioned towards the great grey nothingness outside, not fog, not landscape, but what John Milton (13 handicap) once called 'not light but darkness visible'. I hopped off into what might very well have been the edge of the world, as it was conceived by those Portuguese mariners who would have liked very much to discover America but who were afraid to sail out into the Atlantic, beyond sight of land, for fear of falling off. The word, God knows how it got through, was that Donald Steel* was doing nicely towards repeating his win of the previous year. He had just teed off on the second nine. I ran into a swirl of nothingness and, sure enough, there emerged, like a zombie on the heath in a horror film, a plumpish, confident figure recognisable at three yards as Steel. He took out an iron for his approach shot, though what he thought he was approaching I have no idea – San Salvador, no doubt. He hit it low and clean, and a sizeable divot sailed away from him and vanished. He went off after it and vanished too. I kept following in the gloom, and from time to time a wraith swinging a golf club would loom up, take two steps and be gone.

* Donald Steel (b. 1937): distinguished golf-course designer, amateur golfer and golf writer. Played in the Open in 1970 and also selected for the Home Internationals in the same year. Won the President's Putter at Rye three times.

It was true! They all finished, and nobody lost a ball. I felt my way back to the clubhouse, and at the end the last ghost was in. Within five minutes they were up against the bar, chests out, faces like lobsters, beer mugs high, slapping thighs, yokking it up. Queer fish, the Oxford and Cambridge Golfing Society. They behave just as if they'd been out for a round of golf. What they play every year on that barren fork of Sussex that reaches out to the Channel, and Holland, and eventually the Bering Strait, is a wholly new game: Invisible Golf.

13

Marching Orders

1993

Once every year, the San Francisco Golf Club holds what it calls 'A Day of British Golf'. The idea is to reproduce as faithfully as memory can recall the procedures, prohibitions, quirks and folkways that were peculiar to amateur golf in Britain in its heyday. Not all these prescriptions have been filled in the past, but the hope is that they will provide an ideal which the club will strive to realise in all future battles of Britain. (I ought to say that in the matter of dress, the younger generation of British golfers has by now shamelessly violated the traditions of their fathers – the baggy grey flannels, the rumpled shirt – and gone berserk in puce slacks, canary-yellow shirts and grossly patterned sweaters in many colours; even, I'm afraid, sometimes flaunting baseball caps worn backwards, in the lamentable manner of William Jefferson Clinton, 42nd President of the United States.)

Handicaps:
Two weeks before the tournament, each participant shall be required to post his three best scores of the preceding year. The average of these shall be deemed to be his true handicap. The handicaps of club members posted on the board shall be declared inoperative for the Day of British Golf.

Before the Day:
- The showers must be locked. The adjoining washroom must be swept clean of all its hair lotions, unguents, perfumes, deodorants, toiletries, brushes and combs.
- All clean towels must be removed.

- One lavatory may be left open. Behind the door, a nail (preferably rusty) should be installed, and on it a hand towel should be hung. To get the right atmosphere, it would be well to have the towel hang there, and be freely used, for about a week.
- A well-worn nail brush should be chained to the faucet of the wash basin.

On the Day:

- The Practice Range must be closed.
- All caddies must be given the day off.
- No carts (motor carts) will be allowed. Players must either drag a handcart (which will be called, as loudly as possible, a trolley) or carry their clubs in a canvas bag.
- Matched sets of clubs are prohibited.
- Baseball caps and visors are prohibited (see above).
- Any member arriving in a suit and changing at the club into golfing clothes shall be disqualified. He may, however, use the locker room to change from his regular shoes into golf shoes (sneakers would be preferable). And, of course, he may drop his jacket on to a bench.
- Club ties, however greasy, must be worn in the grill room, but not at the bar. If a club tie has to be purchased, a smear of egg yolk before leaving home will suffice.
- The player's dress should be conservative and suitably dingy. Folded turn-ups on the trousers are not essential but add an authentic touch. Bicycle clips – worn as if from forgetfulness – tap many a mellow memory. Headgear may be either a cap or a fedora ('trilby') with the brim turned down. Tam-o'-shanters are strictly prohibited: they are worn only by Americans visiting Scotland.
- The pro shop shall provide (for a fee) wax tees instead of wooden ones.

The Game:

- The fairways will not have been cut for a week. The rough will have been allowed to grow waist-high (measured by the waist of the tallest member).
- No four-balls will be allowed. The game of golf will be played

i.e. foursomes, sometimes whimsically known in the United States as 'Scotch foursomes'.

- Putts closer than six feet shall be defined as 'gimmes' or – 'This one all right?'

- Marshals posted at suitable intervals shall reprimand all players crying: 'Go, ball, go!' – 'Cut!' – and 'Come round, baby!'
  NOTE: Expletives and blasphemies of every sort are, however, allowed.

- Score cards need not be carried. Each player is put on his honour to announce his final score, however surprising the figure may be to the opposing team.

The Lunch:

- Many bottles of kümmel should have been added to the bar stock. The choice of any other liquor between nines is permissible but is apt to raise eyebrows.

- All American beers should be locked up in the refrigerator, along with American beer manufactured in Europe and labelled with the names of famous Danish, German and Dutch brewers. For the British Day of Golf, beer should be defined as Bass's Ale, Watney's, Whitbread's, Carlsberg Special, Dos Equis, Tecate and Foster's.

- No great pains should be taken over the provision of a suitable lunch. Since the peculiarly British combination of ingredients (sausage rolls, bubble and squeak, shepherd's pie, etc., etc.) is difficult to come by – or even to imagine – the best thing would be simply to offer a choice of lamb, beef or ham sandwiches, served on white bread (English, but not French, mustard should be available). The chef need purchase only the minimum order of the meats, remembering the American Jane Walmsley's comment on first encountering a British luncheon sandwich: 'I see the bread but where's the filling?'

- English club coffee (which reminds the sharp-witted of the last time they drank – er – coffee) should be no problem, since it is standard in America and compulsory on the West Coast.

If the above conditions are met, something very close to a Day of British Golf may be enjoyed, or endured.

14

Workers, Arise! Shout 'Fore!'

1974

A few weeks ago I was staying in San Francisco, and I had a call one morning asking me to lunch with the Russian Consul General and his deputy. The invitation came from an unlikely host, a friend, a lawyer, an affable and fastidious gent, and a first-rate golfer to whom the great game is not only a major exercise in military strategy and tactics but also a minor rehearsal of the Ten Commandments. He is, indeed, the chairman of the championship committee – and will without doubt soon become the president – of the United States Golf Association. His pairing with the Russian Consul General seemed improbable in the extreme.

'Where,' I asked, 'shall we meet?'

'At the golf club, of course,' was his mad reply.

'But why, why?'

'It is very important,' he said, 'I should surmise that the Consul General is coming under orders, and the whole point of the lunch is to talk golf.'

This was like being invited by a rabbi to lunch with the Pope to discuss stud poker. I accepted instantly.

The co-host was a young American, a boyish type, who is associated with his famous father in the most successful golf-architecture firm on earth. Golf architecture is the art and science of designing and building golf courses, and it involves much knowledge of landscape, soils, grasses, water drainage, engineering, meteorology, and sometimes – I feel – black magic. Let us call the young man Mr Jones, for that happily is his name.

It seems he had recently got back from Moscow, where he and his father had responded to what must have sounded like a joke more unlikely than the reason for our lunch: a call from the Mayor of Moscow to consider building the first Russian golf course. The impulse, apparently, had come from a Soviet diplomat who had been exposed to the decadent West and had become one maniacal golfer. This in itself should give us pause. I should have guessed that any Russian who had yielded to such a capitalist diversionary activity as golf would have been, on his first homecoming, bundled off to Siberia, where he'd have been condemned to play golf with a red ball and a snow sled. But he was a close friend of the Mayor of Moscow. When he returned from a foreign, Western, post, he came into the airport carrying a golf bag. The customs men – as also, I imagine, the military and the narcotics squad – examined the weaponry, but reluctantly gave him the benefit of his diplomatic passport. Somehow the man sold the Mayor of Moscow on the idea of a city – public, of course – golf course. I don't suppose things rested there. The matter went up to the Kremlin. And, from all I could gather, Mr Brezhnev gave the nod.

Well, we sat down to lunch, and the Consul General – a stocky man in the regulation Sears Roebuck suit – turned out to have a puckish humour. When we asked him if the Russians would take to golf, he said, 'I think, because, you see, the Russian people like quick games.' Somebody said, 'Like chess.' He came back on the hop: 'Yes, we like a quick win.' He plainly and admittedly knew nothing. But he asked everything. And to help him with the rudiments – of building rather than playing – young Mr Jones put on a lantern lecture, with colour slides showing rice paddies in Bangkok being transformed – slide by slide – into a bulldozed mess, then into terraced ground, then into ground being planted with gravel and soil and seed, and eventually emerging as a pastoral golf hole. Through a series of other slides we went to Hawaii and Florida and Scandinavia and, in the end, to the five sites around Moscow from which they will choose the one on which to build the course.

After that, the Consul General was given a lesson in weaponry. We went off in electric carts, like a little motorized battalion, to the eleventh tee on the noble San Francisco Golf Club course, a swaying landscape of lush green meadows flanked with towering cypresses and pine and occasional stands of eucalyptus.

The eleventh hole is a par 3: that is to say, you are required to hit the green with your first shot and then sink the ball with two putts.

Our lawyer host, Mr Frank (Sandy) Tatum,* straightened his waistcoat (all *ex officio* members of the United States Golf Association board are very sensitive to the ancient amenities and insist on playing in ties and waistcoats, like the respectable Scots in the old prints). Offhand, I would bet that this Tatum, on that hole, would hit the green ninety-nine times in every hundred. He hit about six inches behind the ball, which rose in an unsteady arc and landed about 150 yards away, well short of a cavernous bunker. 'Dear me,' he said with splendid restraint.

'So,' said the deputy consul (a pretty fresh type, I thought), 'the first pancake is never any good.' Ignoring this gem of Russian folk wisdom, Mr Tatum set up another ball, and this time was comfortably on the green. Now, with many open-handed gestures and facetious bows, the Consul General was motioned to 'have a go'. He took off his jacket, looked down at the ball, gripped the club with all ten fingers (the so-called baseball grip, which about one professional in a hundred uses). His two hands were far apart. He missed the ball at the first swipe, but at the second it fell just a little short of Tatum's first effort. There was general applause. 'A natural talent,' purred the gallant Mr Tatum. 'Please,' said the Consul General.

Then the deputy had a go, and he slithered the ball about thirty yards along the ground. 'That deputy,' one of our group whispered, 'he sure knows what he's doing.' Well, then we all departed for the clubhouse, had our pictures taken, and the

---

* Frank (Sandy) Tatum, as predicted by AC, became president of the USGA (1978–9).

Consul General was presented, by young Mr Jones, with a copy of an article I had once written on the origins of golf. Mysterious, this. 'Why?' I asked young Jones. He looked for a second over his shoulder. 'Don't you see,' he hissed, 'it supports the main argument?' And what would that be? 'What we kicked around at lunch.'

I realised then why I had been seated at lunch next to the Consul General. He had dropped several uncomfortable hints that he knew golf was a rich man's hobby, and I sensed that Moscow had asked him to check on this repulsive legend. I hastened to disabuse him with – young Jones later assured me – deeply moving eloquence. 'No, no,' I said, 'that used to be so long ago, even then only in England and America, never in Scotland.' I painted a picture, all the more poignant for being true, of poor little boys going off with their sticks and paying a few pennies to play some of the most hallowed courses on earth. 'In Scotland,' I said, 'the people learn to play golf as simply as they learn to drink tea. And St Andrews, which is the Vatican – pardon me, the Kremlin – of golf, is a public course. On Sundays they close it so that little old ladies and dogs and babies can frolic – can walk around – for it is a public park absolutely *for the people.*'

'No?' said the Consul General.

'Yes,' I said.

'What,' he asked, 'will our people do, will they succeed at this sport?' No question, I said, 'ten years from now' – we were well along with the vodka martinis – 'I swear to you the British or American Open champion' – ('Open? What means this open?') – 'the golf champion of Britain or America will be a Russian. After all, not so many years ago you sent over a Russian basketball team, and Americans shook with laughter. Until you wiped the floor with both the Americans and the Canadians.'

'Wiped?'

'Beat, trounced, massacred, defeated!'

'It is so,' said the Consul, looking gloomily into his vodka.

'Very well, then,' I went on, 'maybe the big switcheroo will come sooner than ten years. Maybe four, five years from now, there will be a match between the best player in the world, Jack Nicklaus, and Nicholas the Third.'

'There was never any Nicholas the Third,' said the knowing deputy.

'But there will be,' I cried, 'and he will win!'

'Iss possible?'

'Is certain.'

I went back to town feeling I had done creditably on my first assignment as ambassador without portfolio. There were, of course, certain little nuisances: of having to learn to play the game (from whom?), to find courses to learn it on, pros willing to spend a couple of years teaching the first Russian golfer how, for God's sake, to hit a golf ball straight. I thought of Nicklaus, at the age of ten, going on the practice tee every day for a year to have his head gripped for an hour on end by the hand of an assistant pro so he could learn to keep his head still. Perhaps I should have stretched the apprenticeship period to ten or twenty years.

Still, if they get around to building the Jones* course, I like to imagine Mr Brezhnev or his successor, or his successor, standing on the first tee and approaching a ribbon with a mighty pair of shears. He will carry in his hand a note or two from our San Francisco Summit, and he will proclaim to a vast assembly of the peoples of all the Russias: 'So! I have the extremely great honour to say to the citizens of our Soviet Socialist Republics – let us begin to play Goalf! The pipple's sport!'

---

* Robert Trent Jones Jr got as far as drawing up plans for a course near Nakhabino, a few miles northwest of Moscow – one of several possible sites proposed by the Russians – but nothing happened while détente ebbed and flowed for a decade. The course was back on the agenda in 1986, but it took the best part of another ten years to raise the money and construct what began as the nine-hole Moscow City Golf Club and evolved into Le Meridien Moscow Country Club – the only eighteen-hole championship course in Russia.

15

The Inauguration of President Grant

*Speech given to inaugurate Grant C. Spaeth at the
annual meeting of the United States Golf Association
at San Diego, California, January 1990*

You may well wonder what are my credentials for standing up
and addressing the Politburo and Central Committee of the
ruling body of golf.

I have two credentials. The first is that I am the President of a
world-wide organisation: I am the President of HOW – Hackers
of the World. As such, I am invited by the Chairman of (the)
Augusta National (Golf Club) every April to attend the amateur
dinner (which is held the evening before the Masters tournament
begins) and talk to the amateurs – usually from Britain and the
United States – who are about to play in the tournament. I tell
them two things.

First: Do not slight the hackers. Pay attention to them. Be
kind to them. It's because of them – of us – that you can earn
$800,000 a year for merely hitting a small ball across country
into a small hole.

The second thing I tell them is: Don't do it! Don't turn pro! Be
like Bobby Jones. Stay an amateur for life. Yield not to temp-
tation! Be like General George Marshall, when Mr Henry Luce,
the founder of *Time* and *Life* (the magazines, that is), came to
him and said: 'General, I want to publish your memoirs.' To
which, Marshall said: 'I am not going to write my memoirs,
because there are too many people who were involved in the
Second World War who are still alive and who might be hurt by
what I write.' Mr Luce said: 'General, I don't think you understand. I am offering you one million dollars.' And General
Marshall replied: 'Mr Luce, I'm afraid *you* don't understand:

I am not interested in one million dollars.' Well, I tell this story to these pink-cheeked nineteen-year-olds, and add: 'Don't lust after a million dollars. There is more in life than golf.' I always notice from their expressions – and from yours – that they can't imagine what that possibly could be.

So, they are very polite and pay absolutely no attention. I'd say that of the forty or fifty amateurs I've preached to in the past ten, dozen, years, maybe three have made their way on the American tour. The rest slog away on the European tour, if they're lucky, on the New Zealand tour, on the Fiji tour, the Tibetan tour. By which time, they decide to change teachers. They line up with some exotic instructor in southern Florida or the Carmel Valley, and from him they learn that the backswing has fifteen 'accumulated' positions, which must be fused into a single action. If they master this procedure, it does guarantee that they will become the club pro in Four Corners, Colorado, or Little Piddletrenthide and secure the local franchise in sweaters and jock straps.

My second credential far outweighs the first: it is the express invitation of – how can I say *Mr* Spaeth? Who for so many years, at the San Francisco Golf Club, was pointed out to me striding through the grill room, striding down the fairways, striding out of the woods. And they would say: 'That is Mr Big.' Then came the time, only a year or two ago, when he won the – wait for it! – Senior – Amateur – Championship – of – the – municipality – of Palo Alto! Since when, he has been universally known as Big Muni. We thought at the time that that was as high as a man would want to go. But no. He has gone up and up to improbable heights, and now – against all the predictions – he is the President of the United States Golf Association! El Presidente, no less.

Some of you may be curious to know how it comes about that I am not only a good friend of the President and of his great friend Frank Tatum but that I am also a golfing partner of both of them. An absurdity made possible by what to me is the most magical thing about the game of golf: the handicapping system.

Does the name Ellsworth Vines mean anything to you? [*One clap*] Very good. A great tennis player – of the first chop – Wimbledon champ, US Open champ. Came the time, as it must to all tennis players, to retire – in his thirties. He took up golf (indeed, he was on the tour for a time). A few years ago, he said to a friend of mine: 'Golf is the most marvellous game. When I was at my tennis peak, there were half a dozen, say a dozen, guys who could give me a game. In golf, I can play against all but the most abject hacker and have a tough time.'

And it's because of that magical system that I am a member of a foursome that engages in a periodical joust at the San Francisco Golf Club. The foursome consists of your new President – Big Muni; Frank Tatum, known as Sandy. I am known – because of the striking resemblance of my swing to a famous Latino – as Alistairos. The fourth member, I greatly regret to say, is not a member of the San Francisco Golf Club. But he's a dear friend, and we forgive him for belonging to – what the humble members of San Francisco call – the Bloomingdale's of golf and country clubs. It is also known as Olympic. He is a man named Carl Borders. A 1-handicap! Even a shade lower, on the index, or slope. In his spare time, he's an orthopaedic surgeon. Least, he *says* he is. If you call his office, his wife answers the phone. I suspect she is the orthopaedic surgeon. It's the only way you can explain how he manages to play golf six days a week and practise eight days a week.

What I'm saying is: in what other game can a 1-handicap and a 3 and a 5 even pretend to enjoy playing with an octogenarian who gets a stroke a hole and two strokes on the par 5s? You laugh! Let me tell you that the winning side is rarely more than one up. Which Dr Borders and I were in our last joust, and when also on the back nine, *I beat Tatum!* That required him to disgorge four dollars – to me, an event unique in the history of the club. So much so, I understand there is to be a plaque installed up against the only other golf picture or memento in the men's locker room. That is an immense blow-up of Harvie Ward taken at a split second after he has hit the ball. If you ever see it, you'll notice to your astonishment that at that moment, as he is going or has just gone through the ball, he is – like Bobby Jones! – on the tips of all his ten toes. A position which today, I suppose, would be thought freakish if not downright incompetent.

It only goes to show that in spite of *Golf Digest*'s – I think it's now 1,942 – tips, on what is *fundamental* about the golf swing – nobody knows what is fundamental about the golf swing. And so the writers and the critics have to fall back on colourful prose. Thus, a fine English writer, the late Pat Ward-Thomas, loved to quote an immortal sentence about Bobby Jones: 'His swing had all the drowsy beauty of an English summer's day.' (Just for the record, I ought to mention that the swing of the late, beloved, Pat Ward-Thomas had all the drowsy beauty of a pneumatic drill.)

These bizarre facts only prove again that you don't have to be a great golfer to be a great golf critic. Look at me! Whatever I had in golf – or never had in golf – has gone. But I retain my uncanny ability to say what's wrong with the other guy's swing.

Of course, you must realise that for this expert trio to play with me and pretend it's a great pleasure, they have to observe certain precautions. And the first one they observe is precisely the first thing I was taught by my old Scottish golf teacher, George Heron. He was about four feet eight. A wonderful man, one of that generation sent over after the First World War to teach the Colonials how to play golf. Soon after he took me on, a middle-aged simpleton who didn't know which end you held, I became a maniac and read all the books. One book came out called *Square to Square*. I asked George about it: 'What is this Squ ...?' 'Mr Cooke,' he said, 'forget it! Since the days of Vardon and Braid, nothing has evair been added to this game excaipt an aixtra slice of baloney.'

Well, his first bit of advice was to make a point of watching a good swing and trying to copy it. But never look at a bad swing, because it will pass over into what Ben Hogan called 'your muscle maimory'. So the first golf tournament I ever attended – twenty-five years ago, the Masters – I hurried off to the first tee to await the arrival of the heroes. Pretty soon, one obvious hero was on his way, because there was a wave of applause coming with him from the clubhouse. By the time he'd teed up his ball, you'd have thought, from the applause, it was VJ Day. Clearly, a man to watch. He teed up the ball, he swung (golf commentators say 'swang') and he hit the ball. At the finish of the swing, I noticed that his right shoulder was practically on the ground, as if he'd tossed the caber underhand. His right arm and hand were outstretched into the sky, like Adam reaching for God's touch in the well-known Vatican painting. I said to myself: 'He will never be a golfer. If that's what's going to pass over into my muscle memory, I'll be muscle bound for life.' He was a fella named Palmer, I believe. (Considering what Palmer has done with that swing, you had better repeat twenty times on waking: 'There are many ways to skin a cat.')

From this memorable scene, you can probably deduce the sort of precautions my three companions take, in order to protect the purity of their own swings. I've noticed that whenever I address the ball – on the tee, in the fairway, in a bunker, anywhere – these splendid partners look meditatively down the fairway or are suddenly concerned for the condition of their spikes.

Now, you ought to get a picture of what they're trying not to look at. For many years I had an impression of my golf swing, which was: that I vividly resembled Tom Weiskopf in the take-away and Dave Marr on the downswing. Unfortunately, there came a day when I was invited to have my golf swing filmed by a video camera. Something I will never do again. When it was played back, what I saw – what *you* would have seen – was not Weiskopf and Marr but a man simultaneously climbing into a sweater and falling out of a tree.

However, in spite of all these precautions and safeguards and secret vows to give Cooke a wide berth when he has a club in his hand, we all know that the great, the overriding, thing about golf is – companionship, right? They look away, but when I'm through with my stroke they come over, sometimes, and talk to me. 'Didn't see that,' they say, or 'Hit a good shot?'

Well, in pursuing this relationship down the years (that's to say in simply playing golf with the same people) you pick up certain secrets about them. I've picked up some observing your President, and there are two secrets I'd like to convey to you. On the understanding (as I once heard Secretary of State John F. Dulles say to an audience of about 250 reporters) that 'this will not go outside the four walls of this room'.

The first secret takes us back into the mists of time. And what I'm going to give you is a true account of the distorted and sentimental version – of a meeting between a man and a boy – you have just heard from Frank D. Tatum. Let me tell you what really happened.

What Sandy was too modest to tell you was that when he'd been out of college six or eight years, he was the all-American college champ, the idol of Los Angeles's golfers (he is an Angeleno – pretends to be a San Franciscan). And back then, maybe forty years ago, he did have this close friend. And the close friend had a son, a little boy. And the little boy worshipped – St Francis Tatum. One day, he said to his father: 'Father, do you think that I might ever caddie for St Francis?' And the father said: 'Of course, my son.' Came the day, and the little boy stomped around in the ecstasy of being altar boy to St Francis.

Now, we flip, as they do in the movies: we flip through the calendar – through the fifties, sixties, seventies, eighties. And we come to November 1989. Four men are standing on the first tee at the San Francisco Golf Club. My partner, the wizard doctor (who calls himself, anyway, a doctor) – Dr Borders – turns and says, 'Sandy, what's your handicap?' Sandy truthfully replies: 'Five.' The doc now turns to the little boy, who is now a very big boy, and says 'Grant, handicap?' And Grant says: 'Three.' I want to tell you: Tatum is such a gentleman that the spasm of pain, the wince he emitted from his lips, was no more audible than an approaching hurricane. This might have been a short story by Maugham, or – better – by Thomas Hardy. It would have been called: *The Revenges of Time*.

The second secret. When I took up this game, at an age about five years beyond the age of anyone present, I soon deduced that most golfers were – Midwestern, decent, upstanding, buddy-boy, knee-jerk Republicans. A suspicion that was confirmed several years later when I found myself in the locker room at Augusta (I was just there hailing my peers – 'Hullo, Gene, hi Jack, Arnie') and I ran into two journalists who were interviewing the leading money winner of the year. Just then, Tom Watson had won his first tournament, I believe. One of the reporters said to the pro (who shall be unmentionable): 'Frank,' he said, 'is this Watson a comer-good?' And Frank the Unmentionable said: 'Sure, he's good. He may be very good. Of course, he's a kook.' 'A what?' 'A kook.' 'How so?' 'Well,' said Frank, 'first of all, he's a Democrat. How kooky can you get!?'

Well, the word I have to pass on to you is that your new President is a kook. And as for his friend Tatum, he once voted for John Anderson! He is a Super Kook. As for me, in spite of my having, for fifty years, watched American presidents and American politics, as a foreign correspondent, and being renowned (I'm told) for my amazing ironclad objectivity, at the same time, when I find myself in the privacy, I may say the closet, of the polling booth, I tend, from time to time, to be a closet kook.

So, it's a personal pleasure and privilege for me to pay tribute to not only the second member of the San Francisco Golf Club to become your President but also the second kook. I leave you, though, with the assurance, which I'm sure Grant will confirm, that *nevertheless* – some of our best friends are Republicans.

16

Player's Puritan Victory

1965

At Creve Coeur, Missouri, last evening Gary Player, the dapper little perfectionist from South Africa, defeated Kelvin Nagle, of Australia, by three strokes (71 to 74) in the play-off of the United States National Open Championship in which on Sunday both men had finished with a 282 for the regulation seventy-two holes, only 2 over par.

When they came to the ninth tee in the long, silver light of a hot afternoon, Player was five strokes ahead and scrutinising every lie like a laboratory technician with a blood sample. Some of the six or seven thousand people who had padded along the enormous fairways of the Bellerive Country Club decided it was all over, and they had to be shushed as they stomped off home while Player was crouching for his twitchy address.

But all those who had played and the millions who had watched the four previous days were haunted by the pitfalls, the canyons, the rearing forests, the House-of-Nonsense surprise of this youngest and longest (7,191 yards) course in the history of the Open. They recalled the absurdity of the short sixth, a water hole, where on Friday thirty-odd giants had clouted into the pond, thus causing the memorable crack in the clubhouse, 'Let's go down to the sixth and see how the other half drowns.'

They remembered the misery of their idols with the short sixteenth, which has a green as elevated as a pulpit. They had seen great professionals reduced to weekend hackers by the 606-yard province known as the seventeenth, whose great flanks slope down to water all the way. They would never forget that for the first time in eight years the lordly Arnold Palmer had failed to make the cut and after two days was home in Pennsylvania gawping at his television set, even as you and I.

And Nicklaus? Didn't the *Guardian* man say that the 1965 Open 'might well usher in the Age of Nicklaus'? Well, when the Masters' champion was sixteen shots behind the leaders some time on the third day they decided to postpone the Age of Nicklaus.

And also, if the bored ones needed an extra come-on, there was the reminder that Player had seemed to have the championship in his hand on Sunday when he fumbled into a double bogey. So most of the crowd waited, and it was a long, long wait. For Gary Player won this time by never taking a pitch or a putt or an intrusive blade of grass for granted.

At the end he described it as 'the toughest course I have ever played on in my life'. Its creator, Robert Trent Jones, describes it as 'at worst tiger, at best fox'. The forty-odd groaning professionals in the locker room describe Mr Jones as Dr Frankenstein and the Bellerive course as the Monster of American golf. Some of them suggest that it constitutes grounds for a slander suit, on the principle that it tends to bring a citizen 'into ridicule and disrepute with his fellow men'.

All this became acutely well known to little Gary Player in the first day or two, and the chances are that while others blasphemed he praised the Lord for so many ingenious and soul-searching trials. Not for nothing does Player do sixty or seventy push-ups a day (on his finger-tips), study yoga, refuse to sleep on a pillow ('it is more difficult for my heart to pump blood to my brain'), abstain from all 'sweets, pastries, and fried food'.

To the men who cheerfully recover from hangovers and maintain their pars over American fairways as wide as the Serengeti Plain, and with rough as uncomplicated as velvet, Mr Jones's Bellerive course is an affront to their way of life and a tasteless sermon. To Gary Player, Johannesburg's Bill Graham, Bellerive must look like the green pastures.

And so into the twilight he pondered his iron shots for

minutes on end, climbed hills and knolls and stood on his head to gauge the break of the green, lined up a two-foot putt from the pin and the apron, and back again, and picked up every dew drop or hint of fuzz in between.

Never did hypochondria reap such a rich reward. It made him proud to announce that after the achievement of this life-long ambition ('Even as a boy I would say: "Here's a ten-foot putt for the US Open"') he could now spend more time with his family and less on the tour. It gave him, incidentally, 25,000 dollars, which he handsomely handed back in two charitable packages: one to the United States Golf Association to encourage 'junior golf', the other to a cancer fund ('because my mother died of cancer').

All in all, a very worthy champion, a throwback to the Bobby Jones era; and like the immortal one himself, it is not his careful-ness, or the painful putting together of his strokes; nor even his undoubted nuttiness about yoga, health foods, pillows, and the like; but the simple and refreshing fact that in a game which more and more is engulfed by publicity, advertising, and lavish stakes, he is a gent.

17

The Battle of Wentworth

1966

On a mellow autumn morning in Surrey in the first week of October, a large and rubicund Englishman – a golf correspondent for thirty years or so – saw the boys carrying their white scoreboards above the crowd padding away from the eighteenth green at Wentworth and heard the gasp of surprise from some American latecomers at the news that Jack Nicklaus was four down to Gary Player as they went in to lunch. 'You know, there is already a generation of Americans that has never seen professional match play,' said this rueful veteran. 'What's worse, there is a generation of first-class pros that isn't playing it any more.'

This sorry truth is what gave the three days over the West Course at Wentworth, locally known as the Burma Road, for its twists and turns, a peculiar distinction that has faded from the American golf scene. Not only was there the rare opportunity to watch the world's best golfers make a battle of every hole and suffer the alternation of dismay and elation that is known to every Sunday twosome; there was the even rarer pleasure of watching the collision of character and temperament among the Big Four of contemporary golf as they played the form of it that most sustains competitive tension and provides the fairest test of calculation and endurance. Stroke play, of course, has its peculiar excitements, but, as we see all too often on the professional tour, they can be dissipated by an unlucky splash on a water hole. The obviously deserving hero is obliterated by an 8. In match play, the punishment for a single lapse fairly fits the case, and a cunning assessment of the next hole can redeem it.

It is because of this incomparable quality of match play, and the fact that the choice of the men to play it is restricted to eight of the best players alive, that the Piccadilly Tournament (so called because the sponsors are the manufacturers of the cigarettes of that name) has achieved in just three years a unique stature in the golfing world. It is the only world match play championship. Clearly, its prestige rests on getting the best competitors in sight. So far, the Piccadilly sponsors, shrewdly adding to the challenge of match play the enticements of free transatlantic trips for the players and their wives, riverside suites at the Savoy, and limousines on command, have managed to attract the obvious and essential great ones. This year, only an incurable British chauvinist would have quarrelled with the guest list: Nicklaus, Player, Arnold Palmer, Billy Casper, Peter Thomson, Dave Thomas, Robert De Vicenzo, and Neil Coles.

To an American, Thomas would be the doubtful starter, but the British are quick to point out that he drives as long a ball as Nicklaus and was Nicklaus's goad and most threatening rival in the recent British Open. Peter Thomson, as the winner of five of the last twelve British Opens, was – in England, at any rate – a compulsory choice. Neil Coles, the biggest money-winner on the 1966 British professional tour, has unequalled match play experience and holds the competitive record (65) for the Wentworth course. Even so, the British bookmakers, who are cheerfully uninhibited by the purity of the PGA code, posted him as a 12–1 shot when he was drawn against Nicklaus. So they did also with Palmer's first opponent, De Vicenzo, the droll Argentine who is surely the most accomplished perennial loser since Macdonald Smith.

The four others – Palmer, Nicklaus, Player, and Casper – are beyond all question. Player, in spite of an indifferent year, is the holder of the Piccadilly title, having last year mercilessly ground down (over eight holes) the seven-hole lead held by a Tony Lema playing with superlative grace. Nicklaus is the 1966 Masters and British Open champion, and Casper was the methodical conqueror of Palmer in the United States Open in San Francisco.

Palmer is – Palmer. To the British, he is, winning or losing, still a thing of beauty and a boy for ever. There is, happily, no Arnie's Army in England. But on the first day his carefree massacre of the delightful De Vicenzo, by 10 and 8, recruited one. It was a following of a more genteel sort than he ever has in the United States, but it was nonetheless idolatrous. Whereas Palmer's native disciples go into delirium at the mere contact of club face with ball, the British gave out with low, approving murmurs only after his long drives had found their lie, and when his long putts went home the round of clapping was occasionally punctuated by a sporting 'Hear! Hear!' He was the old swash-buckler again, the 1962 murderer of Troon, never daunted by De Vicenzo and therefore never stirred to wild drives, impossible retrieves, or agonised putting. Nobody doubted at the end of the first day that Palmer was still among the Big Three, or – as Casper is clearly anxious to amend it – the Big Four.

There was much curiosity about Casper. He is well known, of course, to the golf writers, although as an approaching menace in the distance he is still unrecognisable after his dramatic loss of thirty pounds or so. But his workmanlike style and his methodical ploughing under of more dramatic talents have, for ten years now, tended to shift the spotlight to his victims. The British are frankly amazed to hear that he is the biggest money-winner, after Palmer, of the last decade. This year, his destruction of Palmer in the US Open in San Francisco was a legend that had preceded him. And if any further audience incitement were needed, Henry Cotton, the most memorable of modern British masters, wrote a well-publicised piece that picked him as the most stylish, the subtlest, and the most formidable of modern golfers.

So these were the wonder boys from across the seas, and they guaranteed the appearance of a more knowledgeable tourna-ment crowd than you normally see on an American course – possibly because golf is not yet the popular hero industry it has become in the United States, and the audiences for it are therefore as selective and critical as they might be for a chess championship, and probably because the Piccadilly offers the only opportunity for golfers in the South of England to see the masters of the game. This surprising fact is a reflection of the Briton's – or perhaps only of the British ruling body's – traditional devotion to links courses, a preference so well preserved down the two hundred years of the game's history that while England, in the South especially, abounds in lush and majestically architectured courses, like Sunningdale and Worplesdon, very few of them are thought to possess the proper tournament qualifications fulfilled by the sandy wastes, the whipping salt winds, and the sweeping dunes of such immemorial battlegrounds as St Andrews, Royal Lytham & St Annes, and Westward Ho! A visiting Scot, watching Nicklaus calculate the distance of a parade-ground fairway bounded by lofty oaks and elms, recalled the definitive comment of one of his countrymen: 'The only natural thing that does not belong on a golf course is a tree.'

But this austere prejudice is no longer shared by the run of golfers south of the border, and the remote prospect of seeing the Big Four fight it out in the semi-finals was one that would have drawn a crowd if they had played on coconut matting. After the first day, and in the teeth of the firm predictions of the leading English golf writers that Coles or Palmer or Nicklaus was bound to be the winner, the layman's secret suspicion – that Coles, De Vicenzo, Thomson, and Thomas were the rabbits – was borne out. Nicklaus outdrove Thomas, found a new, sure touch on the greens, and emerged with a comfortable 6 and 5. Palmer's recovery of his old control over his power gave him a twelve under par on the twenty-sixth green and provided a dusty answer to De Vicenzo's clubhouse wail, 'Why are you so mean to me, Arnold? I am such a nice guy!' Casper, who, aside from the Ryder Cup, was involved in match play for the first time in eleven years, trusted to a 3-wood and was even more disciplined than usual on his short game. The result, against a Thomson somewhat below his normal competitive form, was a 3 and 2.

The first day's surprise, all the more remarkable in view of what happened on the last two days, was Player's match with Coles. It seemed through fourteen holes that all the fee-fo-fum warnings of the British writers were well taken. Coles played each hole as if he had designed it, and was three up at the fifteenth and one up at lunch. By the thirty-first tee, they were even. At this point, Player's puckered forehead puckered still deeper, and his pioneer's tread was more dogged than ever. Long, easy drives and breathlessly controlled mid-irons gave him birdies on the thirteenth and fourteenth, but on the thirty-sixth tee Coles was still in contention. It was only the luck of a superb second shot to the green that gave Player a par, while Coles denied himself a tying birdie by a putt that stopped on the lip. It was a close shave, and everyone thought that Player would undoubtedly go down before the new (the old) Palmer. With luck, we began to say in guilty anticipation, we might see a fiery replay of the Casper–Palmer duel in San Francisco.

Now the Big Four were matched: Casper against Nicklaus, Player against Palmer. Now the loneliness of match play, which intensifies the conflict of personality, would offer the spectator a psychological X-ray of character that in stroke play is blurred by the three or four challengers coming on behind and the know-ledge that a provisional champion is already in the clubhouse. The Nicklaus–Casper match was a disappointment only in that Casper's famous putting, which the crowd had come to see, rarely appeared. On the morning round, he lost six holes and halved the rest. In the afternoon, standing six down against Nicklaus in his most imperious form, he started the kind of recovery that had made the cypresses tremble in San Francisco and had made a rag of Palmer. He did it with the same unwavering attack, the same wonderfully plotted fairway shots, the same swift and meticulous putting. Nicklaus's response was characteristic. He is not to be rattled by an opponent who walks up to the ball and strikes it with the ease and dispatch of Julius Boros*. His pauses before

* Julius Boros (1920–1994): American professional who won the US Open in 1952 and 1963 and the PGA Championship in 1968. 'Swing easy, hit it hard' was his mantra.

each pitch, his reading of the greens went into an adamant sort of slow motion. He was if anything, more of a monolith than ever – the Nicklaus that breaks by sheer impersonality the struggling human beings around him. Casper is untroubled by any monoliths smaller than Stonehenge. On the front nine in the afternoon, he lost only one hole, the second longest of the par 5s. On the back nine, he kept up his implacable advance, while Nicklaus nursed the halves. With a few more holes to go, Nicklaus would almost certainly have gone under. But the lost putts of the morning were too many to offset a recovery that came just too late. Nicklaus came through 2 and 1.

Palmer got off to a start as brilliant and easygoing as his whole game with De Vicenzo. It appeared – but not for long – that a reborn Palmer would easily dispose of the faltering Player of 1966. We had forgotten the steely pride of Player when he is on display as a titleholder and as an earnest man trailing a comet – the identical phlegm, the plodding accuracy and resolution he showed last year in his seemingly hopeless semi-final with Lema. As Palmer flashed his long drives and pitched with uncommon accuracy, Player saved his stiletto for the greens, marched all around his ball, gave it a vertical and a squatting scrutiny, and struck it true at ten feet, twelve feet, fifteen feet. He one-putted one par-3 hole each time he came up to it. On the twelfth hole, he signalled the quality of the reserves he has on tap. He pushed hard into the rough, and his second shot left him far away from the charging Palmer. His pitch was fifteen feet short, but having watched Sir Galahad fumble his putt he then went into his famous act as a biologist examining a blood smear. After an age of these researches, he stepped smartly to the ball and holed out. Palmer failed again and was suddenly three down. He never recovered. In what has come to be his familiar heartbreaking epilogue to a collapse, he drove out of bounds from the seventeenth tee and, under the miserable strain of yet another squandered victory, forgot himself so far as to drive again, out of turn. Player, with a similar bad drive – his only flaw all day – bounced back from a tree and had to putt left-handed into the fairway. But all he needed now was a six to halve and win. In the dressing room afterwards, Palmer sat panting with disgust. It took an hour or so for him to put on again his face of the Carefree Boy from Latrobe, Pa.

In spite of the puritan relentlessness of Player's performance, most people thought that Nicklaus was sure to take him in the final. It was the worst miscalculation of the tournament. These two are possibly the closest friends in professional sport, but on the West Course at Wentworth, for all their fairway joshing ('What a way to earn a living!' was Player's favourite gamesman's ploy), they were two merciless enemies. Playing a game that in painful circumspection was finer than anything he has shown in the United States, Player first alarmed a Nicklaus who was in nearly top form in the morning, and, in the afternoon, wore down a Nicklaus at his very best. By lunchtime, Player was four up. Before then, there was an unhappy episode that told much about the unaccustomed strain to which Nicklaus finally succumbed. On the ninth hole, he drove into a drainage ditch, officially designated as a lateral water hazard, and was allowed a penalty drop. Addressing the ball, he saw, fifty yards ahead of him and about a hundred and fifty yards from the pin, an advertising billboard with a supporting strut that cut diagonally across what he maintained was his line of vision. He asked for a second drop. The referee, Colonel A. A. Duncan, a former Walker Cup captain and the British expert on the universal rules of the game and the local rules of Wentworth, told him that he must play the ball as it was. Nicklaus demurred, to put it lightly, and demanded to see the book of rules, which the Colonel readily handed him. There was no doubt that Duncan, as engaging a Welsh Guards officer as ever allowed a free drop, was correct in his ruling. Nicklaus did play the ball; he took his wedge, pitched seventy yards short of the green, and conceded the hole. Fuming on to the tenth tee, he commented aloud, 'That was a bum decision you gave.' The Colonel asked him if he would like a different referee. Nicklaus said yes, he would. There was an appalling pause while the loudspeakers bayed for Gerald

Micklem, a former chairman of the championship committee of the Royal and Ancient. Duncan retired, and Micklem took over. It was as if a petulant Catholic layman had insisted on the Pope's personal intervention in an Ohio divorce action – 'an episode', moaned the London *Observer*, 'that has no parallel in the history of golf'.

After dressing-room apologies and a pacifying lunch, Nicklaus came out and for eleven or twelve holes played the best golf of which he is capable. In any other tournament in memory, it would have been enough to crush the closest challenger. But although he was three under par, he was also, incredibly, still four down. Player had been placing his drives and contriving fades around great stands of trees with all the artfulness of Hogan. He was also, for the first time, getting into bunkers and missing the greens, but then he would explode and chip with astonishing precision. And he holed out without fail. At the fifth hole, he marked down his eighth 2. By the turn, the mighty Nicklaus was a spent man. In a thirty-six-hole day, Player's yoghurt, and morning push-ups, and weight lifting, and un-flagging Horatio Alger schedule were paying off. Nicklaus could not remember when he had last played thirty-six holes in a day. He said later that his legs – the legs of a twenty-six-year-old – were crumbling on him, and that it was an actual effort to take the club back. A Nicklaus desperate with fatigue was something that no one, including Nicklaus, could recall. On the thirteenth, he gave his all and hooked so catastrophically that he lost his ball, though thousands searched for it. By then, it was all over. Player marched away as agilely as he had gone to the first tee. Later, before a marvelling, if faintly embarrassed, crowd, he recommended that all ambitious youths read Norman Vincent Peale's *The Power of Positive Thinking*, and swore that during the final thirty-six holes 'the strength of Christ' had sustained him. The secular, and now humble, Nicklaus said, truthfully, 'I don't think anybody living could have played golf better than he played it today.'

Long ago, a wise man wrote the bleak line 'Each golfer may

become what he supposes himself to be.' Every club player knows in his heart this galling truth. He would rather not know the club's opinion of his golf, or, certainly, the private opinion of his closest friends. Each man harbours, on the first tee and in his night-time fantasies, a picture of himself, as he would be with all his technical faults purged and with what he conceives to be the best of his character in control of his particular gift. Once in a while, over a few rare holes or for a lonely and exhilarating stretch on the practice range, he feels and sees this admirable man in action. The moment he is exposed to the cod-like gaze of his friends and partners, only surpassing skill can make them accept him at his own valuation. This secret egotism is surely no different in the great players. But with them the failure of self-esteem is on a more awful scale, since it is advertised to the world and, worse, nakedly revealed before the men best able to judge it – namely, the three or four rivals for the world's championship. Nicklaus on the last day at Wentworth suffered what was probably the supreme humiliation of his golfing career. He is a man almost totally without conceit but of an immense self-possession. He will, with a cool lack of pretension alarming in a man of twenty-six, weigh the virtues against the defects of every golfer of the top flight. These quiet assessments tend to leave the listener with the implication that there is, in fact, only one golfer in the world with the skill and majesty to pass judgement on the rest. He is, needless to say, Jack Nicklaus. One can only guess at the wounding effect of Player's performance on such a characterful giant. For Nicklaus, through most of the afternoon, was about at his peak. The great power, the calculated control of his fairway shots, the prudence that directs his short game always to the end in sight were all on view, and they were, to be frank, more than a little boring in their perfection. For in the last year or so Nicklaus has become more deliberate than Sanders. His reading of the greens is by now almost a private exercise in surveying, of the kind you see done by squinting young men on lonely country roads. The crowd does not rise to Nicklaus, for many reasons, chief of which, probably, is that since Palmer is still the extrovert hero, Nicklaus, the introvert opposite, has to be the anti-hero. At Wentworth, the crowd was markedly respectful but sometimes bored and, after the unfortunate episode at the ninth hole, stonily and respectfully cool. Yet one could sense in the onlookers their awareness of what Nicklaus can summon up in a pinch. Many of those present had applauded his daring judgement at Muirfield, in this year's British Open, when, on the 528-yard seventeenth hole, needing a birdie and a par to win, he made the green with a 3- and a 5-iron. But here at Wentworth he could not begin to break the armour-plate invulnerability of Player. It so happened that Player, as he himself confessed, was engaged in 'the best round I ever played in my life'. The failure of Nicklaus to dent him and, over the last ten holes or so, to sustain the competition was devastating disproof of the theory, widely held in American golfing circles, that Nicklaus at his peak is undoubtedly the best there is. The more approximate truth seems to be that Nicklaus or Palmer or Casper or Player at his best is unbeatable against any one of the others at something *just below his best*. But this was not the issue at Wentworth. It was the best of Nicklaus seen to be futile and impotent against the best of Player. The afternoon of Saturday, October 8th, is very likely the one that Nicklaus, in the tolerant autumn of his old age, will most want to forget.

18

Nicklaus: Twenty-two Years
at Hard Labour

1972

Jack Nicklaus, thirty-two, of Columbus, Ohio, is the best golfer in the world, and he means to improve.

That, in brief, is what sets him apart from the other giants of the game, and perhaps from the giants of most other games also. He first picked up a golf club when he was ten and for the past twenty-two years has been labouring over his game, in the flesh by day and in the mind by night. He is certainly the most cerebral golfer since Ben Hogan, whose *The Fundamentals of Modern Golf* is practically an advanced text on human anatomy and aerodynamics. And he is the coolest, the least fooled, analyst of his own game since 'the immortal one' of golf, Robert Tyre Jones.

'The golf swing for me,' Nicklaus told Herbert Warren Wind, who has written the best golfing biography that has appeared so far, 'is a source of never-ending fascination. On the one hand, the swings of all the outstanding golfers are decidedly individual but, on the other, the champions all execute approximately the same moves at the critical stages of the swing ... there is still a lot about the swing we don't know and probably never will ... in any event, scarcely a day goes by when I don't find myself thinking about it.'

These spells of monkish contemplation are given over to a physical act that takes approximately two seconds to perform: namely, the dispatching of a dimpled white ball 1.68 inches in diameter towards a hole in the ground 4¼ inches wide. The British, an enervated race, prefer to make the attempt on a ball only 1.62 inches in diameter. The British ball balloons less alarmingly downwind and bores more easily and accurately into the wind, but it compensates nastily for these advantages by nestling more snugly in the rough, in the sand of the bunkers, and in the lusher fringes of the putting greens. Nicklaus, at this moment, is bringing his powerful and finicky mind to bear on the problems of the British ball, since next Wednesday he will use it to tee off at Muirfield, one of the great strategical courses of Scotland, in the British Open championship.

It is very likely that the television audience for this joust will be larger, and more breathless, than any since the cathode tube turned golf into a weekend mass entertainment and Arnold Palmer into the first millionaire professional golfer. For, after Nicklaus's win in the US Open three weeks ago at Pebble Beach, on Carmel Bay, he will be on the third leg of a four-lap ambition that has never been achieved: to win in the same year the four main golf tournaments of the world – the Masters, the US Open, the British Open, and the American Professional Golfers' Association championship. In April, Nicklaus led the field from the first day to the last in the Masters. He did the same at Pebble Beach in the Open.

Because he is acknowledged to be the best golfer to have come along since Ben Hogan, and is thought (by himself among other experts) to be in his prime, he began to tempt himself last winter with the heady vision of performing in 1972 the so-called Grand Slam. The phrase is borrowed from the unique performance of Nicklaus's boyhood idol, Bob Jones, in sweeping in 1930 what a sports writer of the day called 'the impregnable quadrilateral'. This grandiose morsel of 1920s prose described what were in those days the four main world championships. It tells us something about the social shift of golf from 'a gentleman's game' to a money game that these four were then the US Amateur championship, the British Amateur, the US Open and the British Open. Jones's feat, done by a 28-year-old Atlanta lawyer as handsome as Apollo and as engaging as Charlie Brown, earned him a ticker-tape parade up Broadway as impressive as Lindbergh's and made him the one golfer known and adored in countries that wouldn't know a bunker from a hole in the ground. He retired, still an amateur, from all competitive golf, and it is about as sure as anything can be that his Grand Slam will never be done again. Today, if any amateur should emerge of Jones's superlative quality, he would surely turn pro in a game which only twenty years ago rewarded the leading money-winner of the tour with $37,032 and today would guarantee him closer to $200,000. Moreover, if a second such prodigy remained an amateur (Jones, for most of the year, was a weekend golfer), he could not possibly hone his game to the relentless modern standard of a hundred or so pros on the tour who follow the sun from January through October playing, on an average, about 150 days a year. The University of Houston alone scouts the country for promising lads, entices them with a golf scholarship, plants them on the practice tee in the dawn of their freshman year, has them hitting two or three hundred balls a day for four years and releases them at sunset on graduation day with the prospect of an early place on the professional tour (and the bonus of a highly 'relevant' degree, a Bachelor of Business Management).

It is against such an army of single-minded young warriors, dedicated from their teens to the glory of golf and one million bucks, that Jack Nicklaus is now waging his audacious, one-man war. Less than a decade ago it was safe to wager that the Masters or the US Open would be won either by Arnold Palmer, then at his peak, or by two or three other giants who were always pacing him, including the hulking young man from Ohio State who would soon match Palmer and eclipse him. Today, picking the winner of a given PGA tournament is about as rational as lining up in one race every winning nag of the year between Belmont Park and Santa Anita and laying a hundred to one. There are at the least two dozen players on the golf tour capable of winning any tournament.

When the golf writers began to conjure with Nicklaus's vision and approached him to name the odds on his Grand Slam, he facetiously guessed 'a million to one'. When he came into the press tent at Augusta having won the Masters, the compulsive purple-prose writers pressed him again. 'Well, now,' he said, 'I guess they're down to a thousand to one.' Three weeks ago, two down and two to go, the racing touts were still at it.

'You name it,' sighed Nicklaus, 'fifty to one, a hundred to one.'

He has, by the way, developed since the early days of his modest fame as US Amateur champion an attitude to the press that reflects very sharply his uncalculating Midwestern assumption that everybody in sight, a president or a busboy, is his equal until proved otherwise. It is the custom at all the professional tournaments for the leaders of the day to retire to the press tent and go over their round hole by hole, club by club. It can be a dull, or funny or embarrassing ceremony. There are the anxious ones who crack the snappy chestnuts known to every Sunday foursome in the land. There are fine golfers who interminably unburden their woes, usually to convey the subtle point that they ought to be leading by four strokes. A few imperious ones, presuming – often correctly – that most of the reporting pack are golfing duffers, exercise the tolerance of Aristotle discussing philosophy with a convention of high-school prize essayists.

Nicklaus's golfing intelligence (a special endowment and one, like an actor's or banker's intelligence, quite unrelated to wisdom, horse sense or even a creditable IQ) used to make him brusque with neophytes. But he has matured in this, as in several other traits, and is now alert to the slightest hint of golfing know-how from any reporter, no matter how green. He warms to cub reporters with candid, often long and detailed answers. Only rarely does he glare in stupefied disbelief at the reporter-statisticians who, year in year out, think of golf as a bucolic variation on roulette. Five years ago, he came dripping in from the 100-degree heat of Baltusrol, New Jersey, having figured on a finishing 65, having made it, and having incidentally beaten the record four-round score for the US Open. (In a practice round early in the week, he had matched the infernal heat with a scorching 62. 'A freak,' he called it, 'it doesn't mean a thing.' 'Jack,' cried a palpitating reporter, 'if you hadn't bunkered your approach on the second, and three-putted the tenth, and you'd made that short putt on the sixth, my God you'd have had another 62.' Nicklaus looked at the man with stony compassion. In his incongruously squeaky tenor, he snapped, 'If, if, if – that's what the game is all about.')

What his game is all about is a question now absorbing many million golfers throughout the world, not to mention the captive wives and small fry huddled around the telly who are just learning to take the old man's word that the grim-jawed blond up there scrutinising four feet of innocent grass, and whom the gee-whiz commentators keep calling 'The Golden Bear', is also the golden boy of contemporary golf.

Jack William Nicklaus (pronounced Nicklus, not Nick-louse) is the great-grandson of an immigrant boiler-maker from Alsace-Lorraine and the son of a prosperous Columbus, Ohio, pharmacist whose hobbies were Ohio State football, golf, fishing, and recounting to his son the miracles of St Robert Tyre Jones. Jack was born in 1940, the year of Dunkirk and the Fall of France, when the British were ploughing up their golf courses and planting land mines against the anticipated Nazi invasion. (Last month, one of them exploded under an oak tree on the ninth fairway at Knole, in Kent, causing an irritated Englishman to lose his stance and his ball; he was allowed, however, to drop another, two club's-lengths from the crater, no nearer the hole, without penalty.)

Considered as a modern type, Nicklaus's progress through school and college makes him sound like a throwback to a De Sylva, Brown and Henderson musical of 1927. A Midwestern boy so albino-blond that an early golfing team-mate called him 'Snow White', he worked in his father's drug store after school, played basketball, baseball, football and track; never thought of going to any other college than good old Ohio State; made Phi Gamma Delta ('it was crucial to make a fraternity, for the undergraduate who had no social life at all'); met a pretty blonde, Barbara Bash, Pledge Princess of the campus in her freshman year, and married her in his senior year. In the intervals of playing basketball, competing in college or national amateur golf, or fly-casting with his father, he completed a pre-pharmacy course and majored in insurance. 'Corny?' he says, 'I loved it.'

He started to toddle and hack around a golf course after his father had an accident to his ankle. It required an operation and suggested to the doctor that henceforth Father Nicklaus had better forgo volleyball and take to gentler exercise, 'the sort of movement you get when you walk on soft ground'. Soft ground recalled golf, which he had given up fifteen years before. But now, on taking it up again, he found he was something of a lagging invalid to his regular partners and he hauled in his ten-year-old as a walking companion. The youngster got his first set of cut-down clubs just as the Scioto golf club, to which Father Nicklaus belonged, acquired a new pro, a taut, tanned, shoe-blacked-hairy forty-year-old named Jack Grout. Nicklaus, to this day, has had no other teacher except himself, who is probably the more exacting of the two.

So, on a Friday morning in June 1950, the golden bear cub lined up on the practice tee with fifty other youngsters. It is clear from the record that the perfectionist strain in the Nicklaus character at once refined the normal, rollicking ambition of small boys to bang out a succession of rockets. The first time he played nine holes he had a creditable 51. 'My second time out I had a 61. Then for weeks, I got worse and worse.' He supplemented the Friday morning regimental drill with private lessons from Grout. The knobbly jointed stripling began to develop a golf swing. At the close of his eleventh year, he went round the course in 95. The next year he shot an 81. During the third summer, he had a maddening run of eight 80s in a row, and suddenly a 74. At thirteen, he had a 69. At sixteen, he won the Ohio State Open.

At some point along this determined trajectory from hacking moppet to boy wonder he admits that he occasionally flexed his ego along with his muscles. And at such times his father deflated him with a regular recital of Bobby Jones's boyhood record: junior champion of his Atlanta club at age nine, amateur champion of Georgia at fourteen, of the whole South at fifteen, at eighteen tied for fourth in the US Open. 'Whenever,' Nicklaus recalls, 'I was getting too big for my britches . . . that usually did the trick.'

Three weeks ago, Nicklaus became the only golfer to tie Jones's record of winning thirteen of the world's main titles.

The long trail, the making of the Nicklaus game, began on the practice tee at Scioto. What had he got to begin with? This is as good a place as any to introduce the bugaboo of 'a natural golfer'. According to the best players and teachers of their time – Harry Vardon, Bob Jones, Ernest Jones, Percy Boomer, Tommy Armour, Archie Compston, Ben Hogan, Henry Cotton, Bob Toski, and today John Jacobs – there is no such thing as a natural golfer. A boy may have an aptitude for sports. He may have, according to the chosen game, the required muscle or speed or grace or stamina. Assuredly, there are born 'unnatural' golfers, as there are men built like kangaroos or penguins who will never learn to dance or thread a needle. But given the best natural endowment, which in golf would be a fluid sense of timing and a temperament of relaxed concentration, the gifted one has then to learn a series of co-ordinated movements with his feet, ankles, knees, insteps, thighs, arms, shoulders, back muscles, hands and head; a series so unnatural that he will use it nowhere else in life. The golf swing is, if anything, more unnatural than classical ballet, and the training for it is as severe as anything known to the Bolshoi. Jack Nicklaus began the grind at ten and he is still working at it, even though he is the Nureyev of the links.

If there was any luck in the time and place of his initiation, it was in having Jack Grout newly arrived at Scioto. Grout was a teacher with some very firm convictions, one of which, however, was that every golfer is an individual. This runs counter to the insistence of many young pros and to most of the instruction textbooks, that every pupil must be broken into the mould of a favourite dogma. For instance, ninety-eight golfers in a hundred use the so-called Vardon grip, which has the little finger of the right hand resting on top of the cleft between the clasped first and second fingers of the left. The ninety-ninth manages – don't ask me why – with a baseball grip, the two hands completely separated. Nicklaus was the hundredth oddity who was more comfortable with the interlocking grip: the index finger of the left hand securely planted between the third and fourth fingers of the right. Nicklaus has hands surprisingly weak in their grip. Grout let him stay with this eccentricity, and he uses it today.

But Grout's tolerance of idiosyncrasy had severe limits. He insisted from the start on two fundamentals. Since they apply to every golfer, young and old, they may help us all, if only we can absorb them well enough to let them pass over into what Ben Hogan called 'the muscle memory'. Nicklaus avows that his game is rooted in these two fundamentals. The first is that 'the head must be kept still' throughout the swing. Nicklaus figures it took him at least two years to master this simplicity, sometimes under the duress of Grout's assistant holding on to the hair of Snow White's head to make him, in J. H. Taylor's fine phrase, 'play beneath himself'. Anyone who has ever had his head gripped while trying to repeat a serviceable swing will have quickly learned the painful truth that we are all 'natural' jumping jacks. I once had an easy-going friend, a cheerful hacker, who refused to take any lessons on the down-to-earth assertion that 'I simply try to be a pendulum'. Unfortunately, the human body is constructed, with marvellous ingenuity, not to be a pendulum.

Much of the difficulty of teaching, and learning, golf has to do with the rich ambiguities of the simplest English words. Taking the club 'back' is not the same as taking it 'behind'. 'Pushing' the club back is a whole stage of development beyond 'lifting' it. To take an example that prolonged one habit of dufferdom for over twenty years, and mentally aggravated Nicklaus's trouble with his head, there is the routine injunction very popular in the

1920s to 'keep your eye on the ball'. It was a phrase deplored even then by Bob Jones, and it drove the irascible Tommy Armour to swear that it was 'the most abysmal advice ever given by the ignorant to the stupid'. The point these dissenters wished to make was that it is possible to lurch and sway all over the place, maybe even to lie down, while still keeping your eye on the ball. To keep watching the ball as it leaves the club, instead of the spot it lay on, is now said to be fatal. The famous phrase was later seen to mean no more, but no less, than to 'keep the head still'. Golf arguments, even between the best pros, often revolve not around a difference of insight but around an image that means one thing to one man and something else to another.

The second fundamental, which Nicklaus maintains gave his game its early solidity, was Grout's insistence that 'the key to balance is rolling the ankles inwards', the left towards the right on the backswing, the right in to the left on the downswing. Here again, the picture in the mind has been painted many ways. Some talk of keeping the left heel down while 'bracing the right leg'. Jones hit off a sharp poetic image when he said that golf is played 'between the knees'. Nicklaus more recently said, 'if you go over beyond your right instep on the backswing, if you relax the pressure there, you are dead.' And George Heron, the little eighty-year-old Scot who, as a boy, made clubs for Vardon, is still telling his pupils down in St Augustine, Florida: 'a knock-kneed man is going to be a better golfer than a bow-legged one.'

On these two fundamentals alone, Nicklaus calculates he spent four or five years, in the meantime working through the range of clubs for hours on end on the practice tee. He says that today 'whenever anything goes wrong', he goes out and hits a thousand balls 'flat-footed'. He was known, fairly recently, to feel he had played a short cut-shot poorly, so after the day's play he chipped four hundred balls in three hours.

There are about a half-dozen other fundamentals. And the later refinements, which can convert an average golfer into a good one, and then a good one into a great one, can be counted by the score, and by Ben Hogan into infinity. Nicklaus has wrestled with most of them though he still believes he is only an average player of short pitch-shots. The problem of mentally selecting which subtleties are applicable to any given golf situation is what explains that fixed stare and riveted jaw as he plods down the fairways oblivious of everything but the tactical cunning of the next shot.

So, you put together years of daily practice, the putting and chipping and 'fading' and 'drawing' and 'punching' and 'cutting' of a million or two golf balls; the gift of total concentration; the sure knowledge that the only opponents that matter are the golf course – and yourself. You still do not get Nicklaus. These disciplines have been practised and earned by any twelve golfers you choose to call the best living dozen.

The overriding supremacy of Nicklaus is due to what you might call calculated gall, or generalship under pressure. When Jones retired from the neurological nightmare of championship golf, he explained: 'There are two kinds of golf, and they are worlds apart. There is the game of golf, and there is tournament golf.'

Every fine player cracks at some point in the three to four hours of his chosen form of tension. Nicklaus appeared to collapse on the tenth at Pebble Beach with a double-bogey worthy of an average club player. He promptly forgot it. So it comes down in the end to extraordinary judgement, at the tensest times, of when to draw rein and when to cut loose. Palmer remained an idol because he 'went for' impossible retrieves all of us achieve only on our pillows at night. Not Nicklaus.

Standing in 1966 on the seventeenth tee at Muirfield, where he expects to stand four times again this week, he faced a par-5, 528-yard hole, rising for two hundred yards and then disappearing as it turns to the left. It takes Nicklaus four crisp and explicit pages of Wind's biography to explain exactly how he played the hole differently each day. Briefly, on Wednesday, he drove off against an east wind with a 3-wood. The next two days, with a west wind blowing right to left, he took a 1-iron. On the last day, approaching the seventeenth, he had to have a birdie and a par to win, a challenge that nobody but Nicklaus relishes. The wind was a little stronger behind him. He decided on a 3-iron and landed 290 yards away, precisely 2 feet short of the rough. 'That meant I was 238 yards from the centre of the green.' (Nicklaus paces everything out before the tournament, keeps a yardage chart and makes notes on odd trees, church spires, bushes, hillocks, swales, visible landmarks. And when he says 238 yards, he does not mean 235.) If he had been playing the bigger American ball with no wind, he would have instinctively reached for a 1-iron. But he paused and thought hard (always the most awesome sight in modern golf) and he decided to allow 'one club less for the small ball, one and a half clubs less for the following wind, one club less for the run on the ball, and a half club for the extra distance you get when the adrenaline is flowing'. So he took – for a 238-yard approach shot that had to land on the fairway short of a bunker and bounce over it on to the green – a 5-iron! He stopped 16 feet from the flag, decided not to be a hero but to lag it close and tap it in for his birdie. The par on the eighteenth was, for Nicklaus, almost a yawn.

All of this, I am alarmed to realise, makes him come out a hero about as granity and loveable as a Viking invader. In spite of the journalistic tradition of tying up such Titans in pink ribbons at the end of the piece, a practice that would not in the least endear me to Nicklaus, something should be said about the noticeable ease with which he matured out of his twenties. He was not always 'The Golden Bear' to the crowds. In the days of Palmer's supremacy, he padded along behind Arnie and his howling 'army' stolid and unloved, and often applauded only when he barely missed a splendid putt. He bore these outrages with great grace, and occasional clenched teeth. He has only lately gained the affection, as well as the awe, of the following crowd. In a country that overrates the sporting swinger and the fairway comedian, he has refused, under considerable outside pressure, to improvise a public image. For his health's sake, and for his much improved appearance, he took off twenty pounds and is unlikely ever again to be jeered at, by some other idol's 'army', as 'the Kraut' or 'Fatso'. In a passing bow to the 1970s, he sprouted sideburns and acquired an extra tumble or two of Byronic locks.

Otherwise, he is simply a mature and relaxed version of what he always was: a Midwestern boy of remarkable candour, quick wits, a pleasant touch of self-deprecating humour, and an unflagging devotion to the traditions and courtesies of golf. All that is formidable about him is what has put him where he is. The unwavering industry to improve his game. His refusal to know that he knows. His iron self-discipline. And the really terrifying self-confidence, which rarely nowadays sharpens into cockiness, of a golfer who is only uncomfortable when he is leading a tournament. He is probably the only great golfer alive, or dead, who could honestly have meant what he said to an English friend who casually asked him what was his idea of the most rousing prospect in golf: 'Three holes to go, and you need two pars and a birdie to win.'

19

The Heat On for Arnie & Co.

1968

It was 102 degrees and the wet winds from the Gulf of Mexico were drenching everybody from the eyebrows to the balls of the feet, when Arnold Palmer pulled a long-iron into the small Sahara of a bunker on the eighteenth hole of the Pecan Valley Country Club in San Antonio, Texas.

A long, low groan fanned over this mangrove swamp, in which the Professional Golf Association of America chose, God knows why, to play its fiftieth annual tournament. The groan came from Arnie's panting army, which through the long summer of his discontent has made more agonised sounds than the French going home from Moscow.

But Arnold had birdied the seventeenth hole and on the previous two he had been within a whisker of sinking two birdie putts that would have evened his score for three rounds and put him in the lead for the only one of the Big Four championships (the Masters, the US Open, the British Open, and the PGA) he has never won.

Now he loped down the fairway with wet circles under the arms of his flypaper shirt, and smaller rings in the wrinkles of his forehead. He looked at the poached egg of his ball in the deep sand. Wearily he took a mid-iron.

It was 120 yards to the flag and offered the sort of preposterous recovery that Palmer in the old, audacious days would have gone for and got. He mimicked the necessary lazy swing and the quick break of the wrists. He dropped his head and took a bead on the invisible rim of the poached egg. And he blasted.

The egg ballooned into a glistening white ball and it shot from a barrage of white sand and took a low trajectory over the intervening rough and the concrete fairway and the coarse fringe and it bounced on the green and plopped into the hole against the flag and rebounded an inch beyond the rim.

The empty sky was filled with a roar, the like of which has not been heard since he birdied the ninth hole at San Francisco two years ago in the US Open, and was seven strokes up at the turn. Palmer was Arnie again, the duffer's idol who makes the kind of recovery the duffer makes in dreams.

It was enough to send him into an ocean of cheering and put him at the start today only two strokes behind the taut little gorilla known as Marty Fleckman and Frank Beard, the spectacled swinger – the new generation to whom a long, hot summer is the name of the game and Palmer is an old hero about to be buried in the record books.

Nothing has been more obvious or more comfortable to forget, in the recent US Open at Rochester, and the current joust in the pecan country, than the muscular youngsters knocking on the door of the fortress where Palmer and Nicklaus and Casper live. Lee Trevino, the young Mexican, turned Rochester into a pop Waterloo, where the old guard with their long arcs and basic swings and all the panoply of the classic strategy were put to rout by an upstart with a baseball swing, a gabble of jokes and a ditch-digger's putting stroke.

Just behind Trevino was Bert Yancey, the last walking ghost of Bobby Jones, maintaining to the end the beautiful turn, the pause at the top, the falling right shoulder and the graceful sweep through that is now about to be anachronised before an onslaught of young guys with the forearms of apes who ram the ball into the air and rap it into the hole and know one thing and one thing well: that whether you slug or scramble, the low score takes the moneybag.

To this historic breakthrough there was added yesterday, and the day before, and again today, the needle of the heat. It turned the knife in the wound of the oldsters' humiliation. Julius Boros, looking like a whipped Arab general, missed a putt of three inches and almost slumped into the hole after it. Tall, calm Weiskopf blew up at a news photographer.

Palmer had a blinding headache on Friday and sent out for a hat: 'Not, for God's sake, a visor' – he still has some pride left and a baseball visor is for baseball players. Yesterday Palmer had 'puffy hands' and other veterans complained that in their greasy hands the club felt no firmer than a snake.

There was a general call for salt tablets, and Trevino, who thrives on sweat as a Scotsman on a keen east wind, grabbed a pill just for the heck of it. He threw up. Never heard such nonsense. He went back to his usual therapy of quick, short strides and incessant gags, and his usual tactic of missing the greens, shovelling up the short pitches, and ramming home the long putts.

And where does this get him against Palmer's graceful heroics? Identical score, that's where: 212, two strokes off the lead.

At the blistering end of the day when there was no wind at all, and the sun glowered like an approaching comet, the youngsters heaved and chuckled around the locker room, and the traditional heroes went for footbaths and their memories were of mellower days and a slower pace.

Today is Palmer's great chance to retrieve the game for the old guard. If he fails,* he might well imitate the memorable San Francisco millionaire, a dogged old golfer, who pulled his drive, topped his wood shot, fluffed in the bunker, and took a small divot on the putting green! He straightened up and looked at his towering companions in utter amazement.

'What am I doing?' he cried, 'I don't *have* to do this. I'm a rich man!'

---

* He did. Boros, aged forty-eight, edged out Palmer and Bob Charles by a stroke.

20

The American Tour
Progress Report

1978

The only Hollywood feature film ever devoted to the life of a famous golfer – if you missed it, may I say speaking with great restraint that it was an appalling film – was about Ben Hogan. Its only virtue was its title. It was called *Follow the Sun* – which does tell you right away why professional golf is played practically all the year round in America, and where the season is bound to begin. In the Southwest, the farthest reaches of what they call The Sun Belt.

It starts in January in Arizona and then goes to Southern California and out to Hawaii. The only interruption in this sun-drenched routine is the Bing Crosby, played in Northern California, and not infrequently in drenching rain and roaring winds. But mostly it's desert golf. And the aficionados don't get too worked up about the early heroes of the tour – one year, it's Johnny Miller, another it's Hubert Green, or Tom Watson. The fact is – as the pros themselves are the first to admit – that hot streak in the desert is rarely a sign of who is going to dominate the game later on. Because, in the desert, there is little rough, the baked fairways give a handsome carry, and the greens are so well watered that it's like pitching horseshoes into a swamp. In other words, it's target golf.

As winter begins to wane the golfers move cautiously north – from the coast and the desert into the Colonial South – first into the Carolinas, and then in the first week in April into Augusta and the Masters. That is when we see the first parade of the stars. It is the first test which separates the good from the great or potentially great. And that's when the knowing fans begin to guess at the identity of the golfer of the year: the man who can weather, or dominate, the majors: first the Masters in April, then the US Open in June, the British Open in July, and the American PGA in August.

Every year, the week before the Masters, everybody begins to speculate on Jack Nicklaus's chances of making the one and only grand slam by winning all four. This is ridiculous – Nicklaus's chances have been figured at 448 to one against. But it is a tribute to the unprecedented hold on the game of one man. Bobby Jones dominated the game for five years, Hogan for four, Palmer for four or five, Nicklaus has dominated it for fourteen years, and – at thirty-eight – he is surely approaching the twilight of his astounding career.

Well, the speculation was dashed for yet another year by Nicklaus's performance at Augusta. On the fourth day, I ran into old Paul Runyan,* and he said: 'D'you know who's been playing the best golf from tee to green?' We all guessed wrong. 'Nicklaus,' he said, 'for fifty-four holes, he's missed the green twice.' Alas, on the greens he lost his touch, and his rally on the last day was too little and too late. What we saw – what I hope you saw at Augusta – was the magical surge of Gary Player who, oddly, had listened to his wife for the first time in his life. 'You're not finishing your putting stroke,' she told him. He accordingly started to finish it, and he proceeded to win the Masters, the Tournament of Champions and the Houston Open – three formidable tournaments on forbidding courses. Obviously, the resurrection of Gary Player, at forty-two, is the dazzling feature of the tour as it comes to the end of its first four months.

Now, we tread water impatiently before the plunge into Ohio, and the Memorial Tournament on the great course Nicklaus designed. That's on the 18th of May. After that, of course,

---

* Paul Runyan (1908–2002): American golfer, teacher and writer. Won twenty-nine times on the PGA Tour and wrote *The Short Way to Lower Scoring*.

we turn to the scene of Palmer's tremendous victory in 1960, at Cherry Hills, the mile-high course in Denver, where, once again, the US Open is being played. And after that, we'll be biting our lips for July and the British Open on the course which Nicklaus considers the sacred ground of golf, the place he'd rather win than anywhere: St Andrews.

It's become extremely foolish even to guess at the likely winners of the remaining Big Three majors. There has never been a time when there were so many first-rate youngsters on the tour. Any week, one or two or three of them will catch fire. The chances of a veteran conquering the hot streak of any one of, say, twenty or thirty players are slimmer than they've ever been. We can only say – at this stage in the season – that we marvelled at Nicklaus's brilliant start – second, then first, then second, then first; then, even this marvel was dimmed by the sustained brilliance of Player over three weeks. But if you were to ask me who's likely to win the US Open and/or the British Open, I'd have to say: watch out for Kratzert, and Hinkle, and Twitty, and Green, and Bean, and McGee, and Andy North, and Jerry Pate and Mike Morley and Fuzzy Zoeller, and about a dozen others. Don't, of course, forget Hale Irwin (never forget Hale Irwin) or Player or Trevino – and – what's the name again? – Nicklaus.*

* AC called well. The 1978 US Open was won by Andy North, while Jack Nicklaus went on to win his third – and final – British Open at St Andrews.

21

The Curtis Cup

1974

When you consider that women's golf goes back at the latest to Mary, Queen of Scots (who celebrated her husband's death at the hands of her lover by playing a spanking round at Seton), it is odd that nobody thought of donating a trophy for women in international competition until the Misses Harriot and Margaret Curtis, of Boston, had the bright idea in 1932. They were both US Amateur champions, and they started their biennial tournament with the aim of encouraging 'friendly competition between the women of all nations'. The response from the women of all nations was a stunning silence. After abortive advances by the French, the joust became unintentionally confined to Great Britain and the United States, evidently the only two nations that produced enough women gullible or hysterical enough to succumb to the marvellous mania.

The first match was played at Wentworth in May 1932 and is distinguished in retrospect by the victory of Joyce Wethered, then at the end of her great career, over the enchanting Glenna Collett. The British do not care to recall much else about the match, which the historian Enid Wilson called 'the blackest day in our golf'. It had been assumed that the Americans would have an uphill time, since they were unused to foursome pairings. But they arrived a week before the match, practised with vulgar zeal, experimented with their pairings and, in the result, won by 5½ points to Britain's 3½. At Chevy Chase, in Maryland, two years later, the margin was widened to 6½ against 2½.

But in 1936, at Gleneagles, Britain surfaced again when wee

Jessie Anderson holed a very long putt on the last green, and the match was halved. Thereafter, the United States won with depressing regularity until 1952 when Britain won, at Muirfield, by 5 to 4. In 1954, the Americans reasserted themselves but two years later, at Sandwich, Frances Smith made a birdie on the last hole, beat the Texan Polly Riley and won the match for Britain by 5 to 4. In 1958, Frances Smith again came down to the last hole against Polly Riley and once again snatched a win, enabling Britain to tie, 4½ to 4½. It is understandable that to this day in Britain Frances Smith is thought of as the heroine of the Curtis Cup. For her 1958 win was responsible for the only occasion on which Britain has successfully defended a trophy either in amateur or professional golf.

In 1960, the United States resumed its so far unbroken procession of victories, and it would be unchivalrous at this time and place to gloat over the details. To quote an English precept not sufficiently taught in American schools, 'winning isn't everything'. Suffice it to say that British bird-watchers like to recall how, at Western Gailes in Scotland in 1972, their sweater girl, Mickey Walker, beat our sweater girl, Laura Baugh.

Just for the record, we ought to mention, in as brief and gentlemanly a way as possible, that so far the United States has won 13 matches, Britain 2, and 2 have been tied. Incidentally, the traditional format of three 36-hole foursomes the first day and six 36-hole singles the second day was replaced in 1964 with the less taxing routine of three 18-hole foursomes on the morning of each day, and six 18-hole singles in the afternoons.

Which brings us to San Francisco and the disturbing thought that the fine old Tillinghast course has been prepared, for the visiting Britons, by Sandy Tatum, an Anglophile of suspicious proportions. The unworthy rumour that he made a point of planting gorse and heather and other horrors familiar to the British is entirely false. It is true that the tapes of his planning sessions have been lost or wiped, but a mere stroll around the course should be enough to convince the most paranoid patriot that Tatum has shed all chauvinism, except – the ladies of both countries may come to believe – the chauvinism of the good old MCP (male chauvinist pig).

The Guardian, *2 August 1974*

San Francisco is the nail of a long thumb that grows out of the sloping palm of Central California. The thumb is locally known as the Peninsula. It has the Pacific Ocean on its west, and for sixty miles or so, San Francisco Bay on the east.

It rises through rolling hills of chaparral to a central ridge. Dense white fogs come rolling in, most of all in July and August which the visiting British, including the Curtis Cup team, are always astounded to discover is the cool season.

So, if you stand on the crest of the ridge south of the city and its littering suburbs (which, annoyingly, can be basking under clear skies) you see to the east a Spanish landscape dropping to a burnt-over littoral. To the west, you look down on the lowlands of Scotland, with much broom and gorse and at all seasons a wealth of cypress and pine, well watered by nothing but the fog.

It is in this opulent evergreen landscape that we find half a dozen splendid golf courses, including the ocean course of the Olympic Club and its championship lakeside course, where Arnold Palmer was defeated in 1966 as much by the soaring cypresses as by his tense ambition to break the US Open record of the absent Hogan.

Literally next door is the site of today's Curtis Cup: the oldest golf club in Northern or Central California, the San Francisco Golf Club, organised in 1895, radically overhauled and re-designed after the First World War by A. W. Tillinghast, the long-forgotten genius of golf architecture who is suddenly the golden boy of knowing golfers, as Scott Fitzgerald is of teeny-bopper movie fans.

Tillinghast's resurrection became an embarrassing necessity when the assistant director of the United States Golf Association recently discovered that 'by the end of this season thirty-five national championships or international matches of the USGA, or the Professional Golfers' Association of America will have been played on nineteen different Tillinghast courses.' For the rest of us, it became obligatory to pay him the passing tribute of a bowed head when we saw this year how his Winged Foot course left Nicklaus and Weiskopf and Miller 15 over par at the end of the US Open.

The ladies who will tee off today for the Curtis Cup will face no such subtle and uncompromising monster as Winged Foot, but they will be playing a worthy Tillinghast memorial. First, it is majestic because the landscape is majestic, and Tillinghast had a habit of not tinkering with God's terrain. Where an apparently broad fairway falls away at the centre into valleys dense with cypress and eucalyptus, nothing has been done to save a long hooking drive from oblivion.

On another long hole, the drive must fly low under a crown of cypress fronds to emerge, it first appears, into the Serengeti Plain. Fifty yards further on, it turns out that the only playable ball must have landed on a twenty-yard strip between a mighty tree on the right and a stand of encroaching pines on the left. And so on.

This is not to say that San Francisco is a punishing or even formidable course to first-rate players. To English amateurs familiar with Carnoustie, Troon, Muirfield, or any other fine links course, San Francisco may well appear benign. The American pros who made their first British appearance at Lytham St Annes were terrified into the belief that they were playing on the moon. It all depends what picture comes to mind when some savant declares that his course is 'an examination in golf'. One man's hellhole is another man's backyard.

The course has been prepared by the only 1-handicap golfer on the San Francisco board: Frank Tatum, the chairman of the championship committee of the USGA. Known hitherto as an affable lawyer with a passion for British links, he acquired a Vincent Price reputation among Nicklaus and all for what they call 'setting the Sunday pins on Thursday' at Winged Foot. But he is also a chivalrous chap who is certainly not out to humiliate the ladies by a bizarre toughening of his home course. It is 6,500 yards from the back tees and has been brought down to 6,100 for the two-day joust. This is about the average length of the last four US Amateur championships.

Unlike the neighbouring Olympic course, San Francisco has almost none of the hideously unnegotiable ice plant. It has dry stubble only within the shadow of the blighting eucalyptus trees. It has, by British standards, playable rough that has been extended beyond the tolerance of the older club members but it has added to clumps of Mediterranean heather a stand specially brought over from Scotland. And, pleasingly, much of the rough is now ablaze with wild flowers.

The sternest test – perhaps the result – will rest with five par 4 holes which are severe enough for the longest hitters. Though of unequal length, two of them are doglegs that are always double doglegs for women unable to bend the first turn or carry the first far-out bunkers. But, at this time of the year, when the Peninsula is under a grey umbrella of fog spray, the fairways are dense with dew, and the length of a drive tends to be the length of the carry.

If the British team has a starting advantage, we are likely to know it after the first two holes, which reveal Tillinghast's love of transatlantic bunkers. The Americans play most of their lives out of shallow saucers powdered with caster sugar. In the recent US Women's open, it was often possible to putt, if not to putt out, from bunkers that had felt a little rain. San Francisco has no Grand Canyons but it has 108 bunkers that call for an explosion or nothing.

The Guardian, *5 August 1974*

It was grey skies, nothing but grey skies, for the Anglo-Saxons and Jutes on the British team on the second and last day of the eighteenth Curtis Cup tournament. Only Mary McKenna, the brunette Boadicea from Ireland, managed to rescue her singles match, and that on the seventeenth green. In the result, the United States matched the widest margin of victory known to this forty-two-year-old joust and ended up with a 13 to 5 slaughter.

It is now time, according to well-worn tradition, to describe the splendour of Britain's defeat. But after Friday's foursomes, which were tied at one and a half points each, the raw material for such a patriotic exercise simply gave out. On Friday afternoon, the Americans took four singles, the Welsh girl Tegwen Perkins, filling in for the injured Anne Irvin, scraped a tie, and Maureen Walker, the bonnie Scot, emerged as the heroine of the small if knowledgeable crowd. She was playing Carol Semple, the current US and British Amateur champion, and was two down after ten holes. Then, she birdied a shortish par 3, parred a treacherous dogleg, and parred the long thirteenth to go one up. She held on, with beautifully positioned drives and a rally of serviceable putting, and on the seventeenth turned the knife in the wound of Carol Semple, who had barely tied her foursomes in the morning. So that on Friday evening, with the team score at 3 to 6, the British could discern a sliver of blue sky floating down from sunny San Francisco into the fogbound Peninsula.

Saturday was bad news from the start. The seemingly formidable combination of McKenna and Walker came up against two diminutive matrons, Mrs Sander and Jane Bastanchury Booth, a tiger disguised as a mouse. And this match turned out to be, in macrocosm, the story of the 1974 Curtis Cup. The presumption, which the crowd of good golfers present was very willing to make, was that frail women cannot be expected to reach the greens of the long, and dew-drenched, par 4s and have therefore been equipped by a kindly providence with an uncanny skill in the short game. In fact, most of the women had no trouble with the wood shots on the most brutal uphill par 4s, but putted away on the greens like defective outboard motors. At the end, it was put down to the very subtle breaks of the San Francisco course, and to the hair-raising pin placements of Sandy Tatum, the same sadist who brewed similar agonies for

the forlorn giants at the US Open. One Briton, tactfully unidenti-
fied, suggested that the proper fate for Tatum was to be 'stuffed
in each and every one of the eighteen cups'.

Yet, the Americans, who are supposed to be familiar with
courses on which there is never a straight putt, did just as badly
on both days. Little Jane Booth, a dogged school teacher, was
the only one to redeem the legend that women must pitch close
to the green and scramble pars with cunning chips and steady
putts. Throughout both days, her chipping was a delight, all the
more memorable because it was atypical of the general putting
malaise. In the result it was Jane Booth who contrived an easy 5
and 4 victory over McKenna and Walker in the morning. In the
afternoon, she played Miss Greenhalgh out of all concentration
and chipped her way to a 7 and 6 win in the singles.

The details of Saturday's play are not something that the
British team would want to have explored with any relish. The
general verdict was that in friendly private matches, the two
teams would be equal; but that the Americans, who play competitive golf all the time, are better able to withstand the pressure
of that other golf game known as tournament golf. Suffice it to
say, by way of rescuing British pride, that most of the onlooking
Americans saw a rosy future for Maureen Walker if she forgoes
her present resolve as a medical student to abandon the fairways for the dissecting lab. The hulking McKenna astonished
everybody with her booming drives against the sky, and some
miraculous bunker play, but disheartened her new fans with the
erraticism of her chipping and the slackness of her putting.

In spite of these dolours, it was a warm occasion, in a
beautiful setting, and there were as many glum American as
British faces at the end. For a British win, after sixteen years of
professional defeats, would have sparked the series with new
life.*

* In 1986, the Great Britain & Ireland Curtis Cup team made history by
becoming the first team – male or female, amateur or professional – to win on
American soil, paving the way for similar successes by the European Ryder
Cup team in 1987 and the British Walker Cup team in 1989.

22

Letter to the Editor,
The New York Times

To the Editor:

About the continuing fuss over the refusal of the Augusta National Golf Club to take in women members, even though women guests play hundreds of rounds a year.

Is it not a splendid example of dedication to a cause that – at a time when every night ten thousand children die of starvation, when two continents are ravaged by AIDS, when the western world is concerned for its actual survival – the National Council of Women's Organisations should stay firm in pursuit of its main aim: which is to see that women are allowed as members into men's clubs that don't want them? If the Council succeeds, let us hope it will move on to the next most urgent cause: to compel the 1,800 women's clubs of the United States to take in men as members with full voting rights.

New York City, September 9, 2002

23

The Masters:
An American Festival

1975

It would be neat but misleading to say that whereas there is the Rose Bowl game, the World Series, and the Indianapolis 500, for golf there is the Masters, for this suggests, by analogy, the climax of a popular sport in an annual circus: the pumping brass, the high-stepping cheer leaders, an amphitheatre jammed with a happy mob cued to its roaring responses by a baritone and echoing loud speakers.

No golf tournament is ever like that. For one thing, and a pleasant thing it is, the crowd is only once assembled in one place, around the eighteenth green on the last day, as the last pair walks up towards it. For the rest of the time, it is many drifting little crowds on their way to a frozen stance. For one charm of a golf tournament that television obliterates, with the knowing chatter of its commentators, is the sudden lull of all gossip as a player approaches his ball, and the cathedral silence around every green. The click of a camera is an outrage that interrupts play and brings a Pinkerton man running to confiscate the obscenity.

This is always the great and attractive surprise to anyone attending his first big golf tournament. He has leaned into the tube on many a Sunday afternoon, the silent spectacle of the players and their caddies on the green broken by Chris and Dave and Byron exchanging guesses and measurements and the dollar value of every six-foot putt, not to mention the distraction of superimposed 'crawls' promising incomparable coverage of next September's opening football game and the Women's

World Breast-Stroke Finals in Munich come November. Then one day he gets out to Medinah or Baltusrol or wherever, and he feels he is at some vast open-air prayer meeting.

Regrettably, there are golf tournaments – and mostly the ones named after show-biz stars – that in the past few years have elaborated to the point of nausea their own forms of razzmatazz: a day of public clowning to enliven the pro-am preliminaries; frequent appearances before the microphone of Mr Big to proclaim, with well-rehearsed vaudeville cracks, his total dedication to the grand game; hats and T-shirts and a comical cart advertising the drollery or glamour of the idol; and platoons of busty little girls in uniform flashing grins from ear to ear every time a celebrity or a camera hoves in sight.

But it is not so at the Open championships either in America or Britain. And it is never so at the Masters. What you find at the Masters is a tournament that is unique for three main reasons: a uniquely beautiful setting; a course of uniquely disguised subtlety; and a social occasion civilised more than the ordinary by the still haunting presence of its founder.

The first thing is the setting, which is that of a Southern plantation before Sherman came bull-dozing through. Beyond the well-guarded gate is a long drive through a lane of magnolias to a circular driveway enclosing a flower bed, which sets off the entrance to a modest antebellum manor house. It has a cupola and thick walls of masonry and is flanked by two low-lying wings. Go through this elegant and inviting house, which could be comfortably fitted into the entrance foyer of some of the stockbroker-Tudor clubhouses built in the Coolidge era, and up a short flight of stairs and you come out on a verandah that discloses the same breathtaking panorama which enchanted Robert Tyre Jones Jr forty-four years ago: rolling, swaying meadowland sliced by slim forests of towering pines, and rising patches of ground fringed with azaleas and camellia and misty with dogwood, more like a plantation nursery which indeed it was for eighty years or more before Jones saw it. It was known as Fruitlands, and its hundreds of varieties of pears and apples and peaches nourished the Confederate armies in the first years of the Civil War. Closer at hand is a magnificent writhing oak casting its shadow on a lawn where there are little tables and twinkling sun-shades and chuckling men and pretty women. You can well believe you are at an Edwardian country-house party, at the only golf tournament, certainly, that Richard Bellamy or Hudson* would deign to attend.

This is all very charming, but even the most breathtaking landscape does not necessarily offer the raw material for a great golf course. At least a half-dozen of the world's top golf courses are raw, even ugly, from an aesthetic point of view just as our own country abounds in velvety parkland courses that might sensibly be renamed Dullsville Hills. The pros keep to their own firm opinions about which of the Big Four tournaments the two Opens, the PGA, and the Masters – is the truest and toughest test of golf. These judgements tend to shift from year to year, if only because the site of three of the tournaments is always changing. One year, the Open moves to Pebble Beach, where the boys who miss the cut curse the wind and the perilous carries of the ocean holes. Last time it was at Winged Foot, and the pin placements on the first day alone stirred even Nicklaus and Miller to wonder if there wasn't a limit to a testing course.

But for forty years the Masters has always been played on the same course, and saving a flood or a long spasm of tropical heat, the Augusta National always plays the same, has always the same well-remembered and well-dreaded holes, is always the same ravishing landscape, a slowly beckoning beauty that can never be conquered.

The transformation of a spacious nursery of 365 acres into what a world golfer has called 'the strategic course par excellence' took only four years from the day that Cliff Roberts, a New York banker, showed 'the property' to Jones and suggested to the wonder boy who had conquered all the worlds there were

---

* Richard Bellamy and Hudson were characters in the long-running British TV serial *Upstairs, Downstairs*, set in Edwardian London.

and retired at Johnny Miller's present age (put that in your record pipe) that he might like to build his dream course on it. Of course, they started with supremely decorative terrain, and Jones resolved to wed his own strategic savvy with his affection for the growing things of Georgia. Nothing was imported, like the eucalyptus tree into California, as a colourful exotic. Everything is native to Georgia: the soaring white pines, the junipers, the Chinese firs, the redbud, the white and red dogwood, the golden bell, the camellia, and the azalea (which the first owner's son cultivated and popularised around the country).

Then Jones brought in the Scottish architect Dr Alister Mackenzie, and together they built a course which, at anyone's first glance, is majestic but hardly formidable. There are only forty-four bunkers. Beneath the towering pines there can be pesky but manageable lies, for nowhere on the course is there any rough worth the name. The aim was, in Jones's words, 'to give pleasure to the greatest possible number of players ... to offer problems which a man may attempt according to his ability. It will never become hopeless for the duffer, nor fail to concern and interest the expert.' Jones was a gentle man, much given to courteous understatement. What he intended, and achieved, was a course that encourages the fair player, tempts the good one, ensnares the expert and murders the great. Only once can the course itself be said to have been murdered. That was in 1965, when Nicklaus finished with a record 271 and prompted Jones to say that he must have been playing 'a game with which I am unacquainted'. The following year, Nicklaus got back to golf and took seventeen more strokes, to win again. This year, of course, Miller will have to suffer from the greedy expectation of the fans that he is going to shoot a 260.

What the first-time player is not told about, and must learn to his cost, are the sloping, rolling fairways where position is always the key; and the slick, undulating greens with their almost invisible breaks and borrows. It is possible, at Augusta, to walk around any one of a dozen greens and get wholly different readings from four different angles. Unfortunately, these hazards, when filmed by a television camera high on its tower, are flattened into billiard tables, which is always true of televised golf, causing the duffer in his den to wonder what all the fuss is about when a Gary Player seems to be on a reconnoitring expedition as he scrutinises a four-foot putt. But the temptations of Augusta are so well-bred, the overall beauty of the place so deceptively benign, that the roving spectator is never apt to look and shudder, as he does at a first glimpse of Carnoustie or Pine Valley. And until the last three or four years, before which only the last four holes were televised, Augusta on the tube looked much like any other long Southern course with pines. Happily, they now begin with the eleventh, the first of three holes where more often than not the Masters is won or lost. In fact, this triangular corner, politely known as Amen Corner (until Gene Sarazen rechristened it Hell Corner), is the beginning of a series of six holes that as much as any other half-dozen holes in golf, tighten the tension unbearably in the mind of a likely winner. They are the eleventh, the twelfth, the thirteenth, the fifteenth, the sixteenth, and the eighteenth.

The eleventh is the most cruel introduction to what has often been the decisive last act of the Masters. An immense drive lands on an uphill slope from where the second shot must fall downhill to a small green ringed around by a steeply banked creek. Only a Palmer in his hell-for-leather heyday would unhesitatingly go for it. A contender in his right mind is inclined to play way to the right and hope to get up and down from the fringe.

Successful or not, he now comes to the twelfth, which looks bland and pretty but is known to all winners and near-winners as 'the meanest par-3 in the world'. It is only 155 yards, played from a high tee over a meadow and a narrow creek to a small green that slopes up to a rim of azalea bushes and, for once, some bird's-nest rough. The massed crowd sees in its mind's eye the happy results of a well-struck 5-iron. The best players in the world have taken here anything from an 8-iron to a 3-iron. For there is a mysterious Spirit wind, some fugitive from *Chiller Theater*,* lurking in the cut through the pines on the right. It is usually unfelt, but it can blow in like a Nor'easter, arrest the ball in flight, put out an invisible spectral hand and dump the ball in the creek or the muddy edge, or plug it in the steep bank. From there, you are lucky, as Jack Nicklaus once said, to make 'the best bogey of the season'.

The thirteenth has its hazards too: the necessity of a long draw around a beckoning pine forest, and the urge to attempt a long second shot that is likely to land you in the ditch cradling the green. But mainly, the pressure springs from too much confidence at having parred the twelfth or from a ragged nervous system after making a six.

The fifteenth is a spectacular hole with a blue, blue lake in front of the green, and there are banked spectator stands to provide the proper Roman atmosphere. It is not a difficult par, but after the nightmares of the eleventh, twelfth, thirteenth, it is the time and place to go for a birdie. The question is whether, even after the finest drive, to go over the lake or discreetly lay up. I shall never forget the moment, sparking Ben Hogan's run for a record 30 on the back nine in 1967, when the tiny figure in the white cap appeared on the crest of the hill far away where his drive had landed. He took out his club, and the glint of it flashed the signal to our stands that he was laying up with an iron. Then he stood awhile gazing at our horizon, a midget Geronimo against the sky, and he paced back and exchanged clubs. A man with field glasses at my elbow screamed, 'He's going for it!' So he did, and it hung forever over the long tunnel of pines, bounced on the far bank and on to the green.

But here again, a birdie, worse an eagle, can inflame the ego of anyone teeing up on the par-3 sixteenth, which is psychologically as damaging as the twelfth. It is all water-carry, and there has never yet been a Masters at which some likely winner

* *Chiller Theater*: There were at least two Saturday night science-fiction and horror movie TV programmes with this name. Both programmes began broadcasting in the early 1960s and ended their runs in the early 1980s.

did not register his doom with one or two resounding splashes.

The threat of the eighteenth has little to do with golf architecture and everything to do with the ache in the head of a man who needs only a par to win. It is no monster, a gentle dogleg to the right, 420 yards. There are bunkers on both flanks but a reasonably wide entrance. It is wise not to over-hit the flag, for the downhill putt of any length winds invisibly. Palmer came to the last tee in 1961 after a long battle won. He had heroically recovered four strokes lost to Player, who was home in the clubhouse nibbling at his nails. Palmer needed a safe four, and he could at last relax. Alas, relaxation was his nemesis. He hit a splendid drive and needed no more than a 7-iron for the green. He approached it as he would on the practice green, all anxiety and passion spent. In the result, he cut it slightly and faded into the right bunker. Shuffling the sand, he decided it was too late to play safe, clobbered at the flag, went through the green and down a bank and wound up with a six. This agony impressed on Palmer for keeps that the walk up to the second shot on the eighteenth is a death march. It is hard for us weekenders to guess at what the word concentration means to the great golfers: a trance in which all of life before and after is blotted out. Robert De Vicenzo, in 1968, padded off the eighteenth green having actually tied, but he was so wrapped in his cocoon of tension that he signed the card that falsified his score by an extra stroke.

It occurs to me that, apart from the antebellum setting, a good deal of the foregoing could be written about many other courses which combine great natural beauty with superior strategical qualities. What finally sets the Masters apart is something as easy to recognise as the flight of a butterfly, but no easier to pin down. It is the occasion itself and the small courtesies and customs that seem to govern the running of it.

The tickets are long gone before New Year's Day, since the size of the crowd is deliberately limited to allow for their ease in watching the play. No other course is so accessible to the roving spectator, on account of many natural rises, and some built-up mounds that simultaneously bring into view the approach shots on one hole, the putting on another, the drives on a third.

It comes down in the end, though, to a certain pride in civility which was not the least of Bob Jones's contributions to the game. On one ugly and memorable occasion six or seven years ago, when Palmer's army made life harrowing for any of his playing partners, some slob shouted at Nicklaus as he bent over his putt, 'Go ahead, miss it, Fatso!' The next year, every admission ticket bore on the back a printed sentence, signed by Jones, which reminded everybody that it was 'no part of the etiquette of golf to applaud a player's mistakes'. It didn't happen again.

At no other tournament in America could an official announce that 'in about fifteen minutes we are going on national television' and have the crowd get busy collecting fallen wrappers and paper cups. A small point, but if the public taste demanded such niceties we might in time approach the happy state enforced by law so long ago as 1951 whereby billboards were banished everywhere beyond two miles from a town centre. By nothing more radical than this prohibition, which alone among the fifty states Vermont has had the courage to enact, the American landscape could be restored to its enormous pristine beauty. As it is, in the era of the hamburger palace, the second-hand car lot, and the suburb on the freeway, we should all be grateful that golf courses remain as oases amid the surrounding trash, as the only true microcosm of what any characteristic landscape used to be. And of all the miniature stretches of America enshrined in inland courses, Augusta National is the noblest.

Finally, I think of the most unceremonial daily ceremony, in which the top players made a point of calling on Jones in his cottage. He sat there in his bathrobe in the living room, enduring God knows what agonies, his curling smile and gentle jokes taking the curse off the twisted hands clutching a cigarette. And the giants of the game, no matter how brash or raucous outside, tapped on the door and called him 'Mr Jones' and watched their manners. And when it was all over, they used to wheel him out on the lawn and he would greet the winner with a little well-feigned astonishment at a quality of play he pretended was beyond his experience.

It doesn't help to call it the greatest golf tournament in the world. Calling anything or anybody 'the greatest' is simply a way of bullying your audience into your own prejudice. Let's just say, then, that all this adds up, in big and little things, to one of the best golf tournaments there is, with an atmosphere all its own, and the one that many more of the touring pros than you might have guessed would prefer to win over any of the other three.

24

Movers and Shakers of
the Earth

1976

On the opening day of a recent Masters tournament, *The Times* (of London, as we say in these parts) carried a dispatch from a correspondent in Augusta, Georgia, sketching out the memorable history of the course. Among the many splendid, even original, things in that perceptive article was the information that in transforming a tree nursery and former plantation into what is surely the most beautiful inland course in America, Robert Tyre Jones was assisted at every turn 'by Dr Alister Cooke'.

This is not strictly accurate, as Mr Jones and a couple of generations of nurserymen and green keepers will testify. For some psychological reason not too hard to fathom, I have never bothered to write to *The Times* and refute this clanger. But at the time I was agreeably pestered night and day with invitations to – oh, I don't know – redesign Sunningdale, convert Hyde Park into a pitch and putt, abolish Pine Valley. The most embarrassing of these bids came from Pat Ward-Thomas in the present instance: namely, to write a preface to this formidable work.* I must say I should have thought that Ward-Thomas knew as well as anyone that Jones's co-worker in the creation of Augusta National was none other than Dr Alister Mackenzie, the Scottish doctor who put his indelible imprint also on Cypress Point and Royal Melbourne.

The scabrous truth had better be revealed here for the first

* This piece originally appeared as the preface to *The World Atlas of Golf*, Mitchell Beazley, London, 1976.

time. I have never designed anything, not even a Christmas card. While I'm at it, I had better make what they rather rudely used to call a clean breast of it: until a dozen years ago, I thought of Bermuda as an island, and Fescue* I should have guessed to be a Shakespearean clown. Nevertheless, I accepted the invitation of Pat Ward-Thomas with alacrity and a large dollop of vanity. For it offered a duffer the opportunity to write about golf architecture, something that I believe has not been done before in the history of the game. Indeed, few duffers have ever thought much about golf architecture, but every duffer willingly carries on about the wonders of his own course. Ask the average golfer to explain the principles of strategic design and he will humbly disavow all such knowledge; tell him that he doesn't know the difference between a good course and a bad one, and he will knock your block off. In other words, in a variation on the duffer's platitude about art, we don't know much about 'architecture' but we know what's good.

It was quite by luck that I became wary of this cliché soon after I took up the game. Being a journalist, I naturally fell in with golf writers, and it was soon my good fortune to make lasting friendships with two distinguished writers, and one fine amateur golfer, who wrote or talked better, and seemed to know more, about the mysteries of golf architecture than anyone else I met. Playing some great course in England with Pat Ward-Thomas, or with Herbert Warren Wind in the eastern states, or in California with Frank Tatum Jr, I had the feeling that I was being taken over a Handel score by the late Sir Thomas Beecham. (Often, of course, and especially with the eloquent Tatum, I had the feeling that I was simply being taken.) I discovered to my enjoyable relief that a great golf course, like a supreme piece of music, does not reveal its splendours at a first or second reading; nor, for most of us, ever. Its subtleties will always be beyond us. I don't mean beyond our performance but beyond our recognition.

* Fescue grass is commonly used on golf courses in the USA.

That is where Pat Ward-Thomas, Peter Thomson, Charles Price and Herbert Warren Wind come in. If you are willing to follow them closely, and to forget for the moment your resentment that your own club course has been carelessly omitted from this selection, you can begin to see the differences between the good, the better, and the best. This coaching will not only enhance your pleasure if you have the luck to play any of these famous battlegrounds, but it will, I do believe, sharpen your feel for the alternative shots offered by a good hole anywhere. To the common objection that 'taking things apart' spoils one's pleasure in the assembled object, I can only retort that the most enlightened criticism of poetry has been written by the best poets, and that it takes a watchmaker to be truly moved by the best Swiss watches.

This book is, of course, meant for consumption in every country that plays golf, most of all in Britain and the United States. This reminder exposes a famous bone of contention that is gnawed on periodically on both sides of the Atlantic. It has to do with the rooted prejudice, which the duffer retreats into more than anybody, about the two different orders of golf course. At the latest count, there are roughly thirteen million golfers in the United States and something like two million in the British Isles.

Most Britons, of whatever skill, have been brought up to regard a links course as the ideal playground, on which the standard hazards of the game are the wind, bumpy treeless fairways, deep bunkers and knee-high rough. Most Americans think of a golf course as a park with well-cropped fairways marching, like parade grounds, between groves of trees down to velvety greens. Along the way there will be vistas of other woods, a decorative pond or two, some token fairway bunkers and a ring of shallow bunkers guarding greens so predictably well watered that they will receive a full pitch from any angle like a horseshoe thrown into a marsh.

There is a marked element of national character in these opposing preferences: the British taking strength through joy in the belief that discomfort is good for the character, the

Americans believing that games are meant for pleasure and should not be played out in moral gymnasiums (unless you are going to make money at them, in which case they become the whole of life).

The Scots say that Nature itself dictated that golf should be played by the seashore. Rather, the Scots saw in the eroded seacoasts a cheap battleground on which they could whip their fellow men in a game based on the Calvinist doctrine that man is meant to suffer here below and never more than when he goes out to enjoy himself. The Scots, indeed, ascribe the origins of golf to nothing less than the divine purpose working through geology. Sir Guy Campbell's classic account of the formation of the links, beginning with Genesis and moving step by step to the thrilling arrival of 'tilth' on the fingers of coastal land, suggests that such notable features of our planet as dinosaurs, the prairies, the Himalayas, the seagull, the female of the species herself, were accidental by-products of the Almighty's pre-occupation with the creation of the Old Course at St Andrews.

Americans are less mystical about what produced their inland or meadow courses: they are the product of the bulldozer, rotary ploughs, mowers, sprinkler systems and alarmingly generous wads of folding money. And often very splendid, too. It seems to me that only a British puritan on one side of the Atlantic, and an American sybarite on the other, will deny the separate beauties and challenges of the links and the inland course.

Pasture, meadowland, links, oceanside, whatever its type, a fine golf course will obey certain elementary rules best stated forty years ago by Bobby Jones: 'The first purpose of any golf course should be to give pleasure, and that to the greatest number of players ... because it will offer problems a man may attempt according to his ability. It will never become hopeless for the duffer nor fail to concern and interest the expert; and it will be found, like Old St Andrews, to become more delightful the more it is studied and played.' In a word, the fine golf course offers rewards for the duffer's limited skill; the moderate player senses exciting possibilities; the good player a constant challenge; and the great player knows that only when he is consistently at his best can he hope to conquer it.

Begging the pardon of our authors, I must say that this famous prescription is not exactly filled by all of these awesome seventy. Among the experts there will be furious debates – as, for instance, why should Medinah, a claustrophobia of woods, be in, and the lovely, cunning Inverness of Ohio be out? The members of Maidstone will no doubt mount a civic protest against their exclusion from what the late Al Wright has called 'the three best unplayed courses in America', meaning the three old cheek-by-jowl links courses at the end of Long Island: National, Shinnecock and Maidstone. (My own private conviction is that Shinnecock was designed by Lady Macbeth.)

But all such doctors' disagreements aside, it is probable that a committee of international golfers of the first chop would agree with seventy-five per cent of these choices. For the rest of us, this colossal book comes along, none too soon, to review the history of great golf architecture from its invention by Willie Park Jr, just before the turn of one century to its likely demise just before the end of the next. For in the United States at any rate, an amendment to the federal tax law, allowing the states to reassess land taxes according to the doctrine of 'best possible use', could soon tax golf courses at either the real-estate or public rate and doom once and for all the private playground. In the interim period – between God's rude links and Mammon's foreclosure – there is the consolation for us duffers that the population explosion and public housing campaigns together will drastically arrest the movement of the 1960s towards 7,000-yard courses and holes made only for Nicklaus. Even so astute a team of architects as that of Robert Trent Jones & Sons foresees only a shaky future for the traditional layout; rather, there will be appendages to housing estates having short holes and a par of 60. This should usher in the golden age of the senior golfer with the arthritic pivot but the cagey short game.

While there is yet time, then, let us turn these pages and read and weep. Here are the power and the glory, the fine flower of many landscapes preserved in the microcosm of the golf course. Here are the masterpieces carved out in the eighty years that saw the dawn, the high noon and possibly the twilight of golf architecture. This book may well be, whether the authors knew it or not, a memorial tribute to the game before Nader's Raiders, followed by the Supreme Court, decided that the private ownership of land for the diversion of the few is a monstrous denial of the Constitution under the Fourteenth ('the equal protection of the laws') Amendment.

When that happens, old men will furtively beckon to their sons and, like fugitives from the guillotine recalling the elegant orgies at the court of Louis XV, will recite the glories of Portmarnock and Merion, of the Road Hole at St Andrews, the sixth at Seminole, the eighteenth at Pebble Beach. They will take out this volume from its secret hiding place and they will say: 'There is no question, son, that these were unholy places in an evil age. Unfortunately, I had a whale of a time.'

25

Saying Farewell to a Departed Friend

1983

There are friends of old Ward-Thomas who knew him best as a Royal Air Force squadron leader, a stoical prisoner of war, a bloodshot Tory, movie buff, gallant ladies' man and at all times a passionate golfer so self-abasing that he frequently fought with a 7-iron any tree that came into play. But the most unforgettable memories of him are the ones that have to do with his career as a golf writer. Without apology, then, I set down here my own memoir of him written the weekend that he retired from the *Guardian* (of Manchester), which he served as golf correspondent for over twenty-five years.

It is always hot inside an American telephone booth in summer, and the caller often pumps the split-hinged door like a concertina in the hope of wafting in gusts of bearable air.

That's what the man was doing. But it wasn't summer. It was spring in Georgia, which can be as intolerable as any Northern summer. And he was not making a social call, he was dictating copy to some cool girl at the Manchester end. He was pumping the door all right, but not just for relief. On the outside, close at hand, was a henchman or legman; clutching a bit of paper that bore hasty hieroglyphics, up-to-minute notes on what was going on outside.

What was going on outside was the annual Masters Tournament in Augusta, and the legman – name of Cooke – was trying to feed the latest birdies and bogeys, especially if they were being performed by an English golfer, to the desperate man inside the booth: a hawklike figure with the exact profile of

Goya's Duke of Wellington. This distinguished image was a little roughed up at the time, because the man's steel-grey hair had recently been subjected to a trim by a one-armed barber with blunt scissors, and from the poky strands of it rivulets of sweat were coursing through the clefts and canyons of a face that just then looked more like that of an impoverished Mexican farmer who was calling his landlord in a failing attempt to prolong the mortgage.

No wonder. It was 98 degrees outside, out along the rolling fairways and under the towering Georgia pines of the most beautiful inland course on earth. Inside the press building it must have been 110. And inside the man's booth, you could name any figure that might suggest a sauna on the blink or the inner rim of the crater of Vesuvius.

Imprisoned in this inferno the man was shouting against the clatter of a hundred typewriters, the squawking amplification of the relayed television commentary and the hullabaloo of other maniacs in other booths. He would shout out a phrase, glance at a paper, drop it, curse, bend over and crash his head, curse again, swing the door open and pant – 'Was Jacklin's birdie on the twelfth or – blast it! – the eleventh?' He'd get the legman's word, swing the door shut again, sweat some more and shout out the cadence of the sentence he was writhing through.

I say cadence deliberately, because even in the bowels of hell this was not a man to toss out unkempt sentences or sloppy subsidiary clauses. When the stuff was in print, you would always assume it had been written by some imperturbable oldster brought up on Hazlitt and Bernard Darwin – always the loving delineation of the landscape, the knowing adjective, the touch of Edwardian grace and the meditative close.

He was coming to the close now. He was hunched against the door and I could see him mouthing the words with exaggerated articulation, like a goldfish waiting for the water to be renewed. I saw him chew on a word, wring his free hand and glare at the mouthpiece with his Bela Lugosi face. I opened the door to give him a breath. He was screaming: 'In the serenity of the Georgia twilight ... Ser-en-ity! SER-ENN-IT-TEE!!' He covered the mouthpiece and hissed at me, 'Bloody idiot! She can't get it.' Then back again and saying to the girl, 'That's it, yes, serenity thnksvermuch. Goodbye.'

He emerges, the rivulets having now formed spreading lakes beneath his armpits. 'This goddamn time-zone business!' he says. For the further exasperation of the British correspondents, the Masters is always played during that brief interval between British and American (Eastern Seaboard) summer time, so that the time difference is not the usual five but six hours. Since the climax of any day's play tends to happen around 6 p.m., the impossible assignment is that of describing the finest hour to that cool girl transcribing it at Manchester's midnight.

The reader would be puzzled to recognise in this raw slice of life the lineaments of his favourite golf writer. The alert *Guardian* subscriber might be expected to guess that there has to be some agile hole-hopping, some frantic checking of the leader board, behind the smooth account of a tournament and the planted hints of why it was inevitable that the victory should go to Watson's iron discipline or Nicklaus's competitive stamina. But the reader of Ward-Thomas's weekly musings in *Country Life* must have believed that he was reading the oldest member, a gentle sifter of hot memories cooled by tolerance.

Well, the man in the booth was nobody but Pat Ward-Thomas – one and the same with the *Guardian*'s austere reporter and *Country Life*'s weaver of stately prose in the twilight. I must say that if there is any regret about his talent, it must be that in print he always distilled his disgust at some idiotic rule, some passing vulgarity, into a mannerly sigh, leaving only those who knew him well the relish of having seen the splendour of his original indignation.

That, in its raging pristine form, was reserved for nobody but himself. I see him now, banging away in a bunker at Maidstone, with the sand flying and the seagulls wheeling away in dismay from the obscenities that were rocketing out at them. Any true account of a round of golf with him would require, before publication, more 'expletives deleted' than all the Nixon tapes.

The last Masters at Augusta seemed more serene than usual because Pat was not there, for the first time in fourteen years. Augusta was also considerably less fun than usual. In the press building there were lots of the familiar cronies. But way down there, on the eighth row, there was an empty chair and a silent typewriter. No more the blacksmith's back bent over, the elbow leaning a millimetre away from a smouldering cigarette, the index finger poised for just the right verb. No more the smothered curses, but no more the quick smile, the bottle-blue eyes greeting chums and bores with equal good nature.

There were two things about his golf reports that set him apart from all the others. He tramped the courses when most were settled in the press building scanning the big scoreboard and – on the basis of figure change – tapping out 'he fired a birdie on the ninth'.

And he loved the landscape, all the landscapes of golf, from the ocean beauties of California's Pebble Beach to the Siberian wastes of Rye, from the pine and sand undulations of Swinley Forest to the yawning bunkers of Pine Valley and the cathedral aisles of Augusta. He knew the terrain, and made you know it, and how it shaped its peculiar form of golf, of every county of England and Scotland and Ireland.

When others settled for 'this magnificent course', he pictured the beaches and copses, distinguished an upland from a weald, weighted the comparative hazards of a cypress tree or a swale. Nobody has ever conveyed so easily the sense of being in Wiltshire or County Down or Fife or Arizona.

He will be greatly missed, but not by everybody. Only by those who care about the good earth and its cunning conversion into golf strategy, about the unsleeping conflict between character and talent, about the courtesies as well as the joys of the game, about many small favours and about unfailing geniality to man, woman and beast.

26

Golf: The American Conquest

1985

The first time I played the Old Course, at St Andrews, I had one of those inimitable Scottish caddies who – if Dickens had played golf – would have been immortalised in a character with some such name as Sloppy MacSod. A frayed cap. A rumpled topcoat, green with age. Pants that dropped like an expiring concertina over his wrinkled shoes. His left shoulder was permanently depressed from all the bags he'd carried. He re-lighted the stub of a cigarette that was already disappearing between his lips and tramped off at a crippled angle. A straight drive produced the tribute: 'We're rait down the meddle'. The first slice evoked: 'You're way awf in the gorrse.' (Scottish caddies, like nurses, alternate between the first person plural and the second person singular as a handy method of distributing praise and blame.) From then on, he said very little, rarely nodding in approval, more often wiping his nose with the back of his hand by way of noting, without comment, my general ineptness. The fact is, all questions of skill aside, the wind had risen to a blasting thirty-odd miles an hour. 'I hate wind,' I said. He squinnied his bloodshot eyes and sniffed: 'If there's nae wind, it's nae gowf.'

Such a remark is inconceivable anywhere in the United States, though it is an idiom as hackneyed in Scotland as 'biting the bullet' in America. Not that Scotland is unique as a wind-blown country. Throughout the Southwest, in Texas as much as anywhere, the wind rides free, but golfers must learn to cope with it; they do not consider it – like the fences in show-jumping – an essential element of the game. The simplest explanation, and it is quite possibly a true one, of why the Scots look with disdain on such things as calm sunny days, winter rules, cleaning the ball on the green, and – God save us! – electric carts is that these devices are thought of as comfortable evasions of a game handed down by the Old Testament God as a penance for original sin.

Certainly, it is well established that the earliest courses were designed by nobody but God, and the most unquestioned authority on their history, Sir Guy Campbell, maintains that 'almost all [the courses] created after the advent of the gutta [percha] ball, around 1848, outrage nature in every respect, and they are best forgotten'. This veto would dispose of every championship course we know anywhere on earth, excepting only the Old Course and – just in time – the incomparable Dornoch, to the north, which this year will receive its first British Amateur championship.

Nature, then, according to the Scots, and to many Britons and some Americans still extant, is the only true golf course architect. In other words, the modern game, which originated on the coastal shelf of eastern Scotland, was seen from the start as a challenge, on stretches of terrain that to most other humans were plainly not meant for a game at all. The attested origin of golf might well have come from Genesis; it is at once fascinating and ridiculous.

The tides, receding from cliffs and bluffs down the millennia, left long fingers of headlands that in time were thus separated by wastes of sand; no doubt, way back there in the Palaeolithic period, some Scots tried lofting a ball from one link to another. In time, they found life easier, but not much, banging a ball along the coastal flats. By then, rabbits and foxes had messed up the smooth grasses, and swales burrowed by sheep huddling against the wind made what came to be called bunkers. At some unrecorded date, when the game had retreated to the meadows far beyond the headlands, sand was deposited in these swales as a sentimental reminder of the sand wastes between the links. Little holes were now scooped out by knives, for by now (we are already in the fourteenth century) an idea had dawned on the Scots that had never occurred to the Dutch during their national pastime of banging a ball across a frozen pond at an adjoining post. The Scottish brainwave? That the ball might be hit into a hole.

So a golf course was never planned. It emerged. And considered as the proper setting for a game, a golf course – compared with a tennis court, a pool table, a chessboard – is an absurdity. Considered as a move in the Ascent of Man, it is hard to conceive of a smaller, more laboured, step. For by the time the game really took hold, in the fifteenth century, the land it was played on was thoroughly beaten up by the nibbling rabbits, the darting foxes, the burrowing sheep, not to mention the ploughmen, tramping farmers, and the ruts left by their cartwheels. It struck the Scots, as it would not have struck any other race, that here was the Calvinists' ideal testing ground. The bunkers, the scrubby gorse, the heather and broom, the hillocks and innumerable undulations of the land itself, were all seen not as nuisances but as natural obstacles, as reminders to all original sinners that in competition with the Almighty they surely would not overcome.

But the grim Scots went on trying, using first the old Roman ball stuffed with feathers and then inventing one made of gutta-percha, which bore into the wind straighter and farther. It was left to an American, at the turn of our century, to come up with the modern rubber-cored ball, which the British with surprising promptness allowed as the 'accepted missile'. But from then on, the American influence, in this as in many other departments of British life (cocktails, bobbed hair, paper napkins, frozen foods, supermarkets, parking meters, etc., etc.), has been looked on at first with horror, then with suspicion, then with curiosity, then with compliance, eventually with pride by later generations that assume the invention was home-grown.

Until the end of the First World War, the Americans appeared to have had little influence on the game. They had been playing it for a bare quarter-century, beginning by obediently fashioning links courses on the coasts of Rhode Island and Long Island. However, two of the five clubs that set up what was soon to be known as the United States Golf Association were incorporated on inland courses: at Brookline, Mass., and, a thousand miles from the sea, near Chicago. The best American professional players went to Britain rarely; in fact, the best of them were immigrant Scots. If they made the trip, it was to pay tribute to the ancestral home, as a parish priest might want sometime to visit the Vatican. But, in the 1920s, the Americans – in the persons of Walter Hagen and Bobby Jones – went to Britain not as acolytes but as conquerors. It was an appalling shock to the generation that pictured the regular visits to the United States of Harry Vardon and other established British pros as missionary expeditions to teach the Colonials. Evidently, there was something about American golf that had escaped the British.

There were many things. The Scots assumed that since it was their game, they must be the natural masters of it. The English, south of the border, had come to look on it as an agreeable, if sometimes an infuriating, pastime. The Americans, it was learned, prepared for it as if for a tour of duty with the Marines. The British were taught to acquire a graceful swing; the Americans learned to bang the ball 250 yards and pick up the niceties of the short game later on.

The British retained their loving prejudice in favour of a links course, and to this day the British Open is played on nothing else. But since only a fraction of the American population lived by the sea, the Americans were forced to be less mystical about the creation of their inland courses. They initiated what Guy Campbell deplored as 'The Mechanical Age' by building in our time a great variety of splendid courses, in every sort of landscape, that owed very little to the Creation and everything to machines and money. Also, long before Americans were regarded as a threat to the British dominance of the game, they had been busy in secret, adapting the golf club itself to their damnably ingenious factory processes. The perforated steel shaft, the aluminium-headed putter with a centre shaft, the pitching wedge with a slotted face, the sand wedge. In turn they were banned by the British, and in turn they were reluctantly allowed.

A typical progression, from hugging the characteristics of the primitive game to accepting the American century, is that of the size of the ball. For as long as any living golfer can remember – back to 1921, anyway – the British have played with a ball 1.62 inches in diameter, while the Americans came to standardise at 1.68 inches. When, in 1951, the world's ruling body of golf, the Royal and Ancient Golf Club of St Andrews, publicly acknowledged that in the United States the ruling body (self-proclaimed as such in the 1890s) was something called the United States Golf Association, a period of *détente* was triumphantly initiated by the decision of the two bodies to standardise the rules of the game (in everything except the size of the ball).

It became slowly but painfully apparent that playing a different-sized ball in the championship matches of each country would present a problem, if not an ultimatum. The R & A followed the usual practice of British diplomacy. They thought a sensible compromise was possible, in the shape of a ball somewhere in between. They manufactured two experimental balls, 1.65 and 1.66 inches in diameter, respectively. They were offered to the Americans as a proud solution. The Americans, however, remembering Jefferson and the Louisiana Purchase (which was unconstitutional, and sneaky, but worked), had a better idea. Why not compromise, they suggested, by using our ball? And so it was. The bigger American ball is now compulsory in all R & A championships and in British professional tournaments.

The British manufacturers maintain, against alarming evidence to the contrary, that the ordinary club player in Britain prefers his little ball. Naturally, they want to believe that a monopoly they have held for so long is the consumer's preference. But their day – like that of the builders of the hansom cab – is done.

And so with many other traditions and practices of the heyday of British golf: 1457–1956 (1457 was the date when King James II of Scotland published his famous interdict against the game, which was running rampant throughout his kingdom, threatening the national security by seducing the young from their archery practice). I pick 1956 as a watershed, tilting the game once and for all towards the American shore, because it was the year when a Chicago advertising man, one Walter Schwimmer, being pressed by friends to polish up his escutcheon by getting into 'cultural' television, mortified them by dismissing ballet and drama as fringe benefits. He voiced the odd opinion that most people 'want to see somebody doing expertly what they do badly'. He thought bowling and/or golf would be just the thing. He set up a golf game between Sam Snead and Cary Middlecoff and sold it to ABC.

After Schwimmer, the deluge. A surge in the game's popularity, not least among non-players. A greatly expanded pro tour. The emergence of golf heroes as recognisable as film stars, dogged immediately by lawyers and ten-percenters able to coax a troop of sponsors into disbursing undreamed-of monetary rewards. In 1947, Jimmy Demaret* topped the pros' money list at $28,000. In 1984, Tom Watson's take on the tour was $476,260, a useful supplement to the larger income to be derived from his television commercials. Inevitably, the potential pro, who once learned his game in the caddie shack, now learns it on a university golf scholarship. And the first-rate amateur, once he has picked up his degree (appropriately in Business Management), is determined to turn into a millionaire pro as soon as possible.

In the running, and financial exploitation, of their own pro tour, the British, in concert with the Europeans, are not far behind. But we are talking mainly about the changes in the amateur game, as it is played in Britain by something like

* Jimmy Demaret (1910–1983): American golfer who won the Masters in 1940, 1947 and 1950. Also played in two Ryder Cup teams. Noted for his colourful clothing, though nowadays he probably wouldn't stand out too much on the course.

2.5 million, in the United States by fourteen million and still rising.

Well, much has changed but much remains. The most noticeable departure from the old British game has to do with its surrender to the watering of the putting greens. As long ago as the 1940s Bobby Jones lamented that the British adoption of what he called 'the soggy American green' would see the end of the necessary run-up shot, whereby the ball is punched to run almost as far along the ground and on the green as it had flown through the air. And it is true that today, except on the wind-skimmed greens of Scotland, the American 'target' golfer can hit a high long-iron approach on a British course with the near-certainty that the greens will receive the ball from any angle and hold it, if not quite like a horseshoe tossed into a marsh. (Still, the British Open has never been won by a high-flying American who has not mastered the run-up shot.)

There are, however, three immemorial characteristics of British golf that amaze Americans and pass unnoticed by Britons, since they are accepted as ordinary facts of life: the club-house; the Secretary; the foursome. The sturdiest of these relics is the British clubhouse, which nowhere remotely resembles the Intercontinental Hotel look of, say, the Westchester Country Club or the Spanish grandee's castle of Seminole. Except on Johnny-come-lately courses, the British clubhouse is a lumbering Edwardian structure, hallowed with wicker or worn, lumpy leather chairs, a rug installed before the Boer War, and a locker room, with no lockers, that Americans are apt to confuse with a cell in a maximum-security prison.

The stone floors, the scuffed benches, the leaky faucet, the pre-war nail brush (on a chain) so upset British golfers with much experience of America that the late Stephen Potter suggested, as a ploy of 'Transatlantic Guest Play', that the British host, off-handedly apologising for the simplicity of it all, should say: 'At least, no danger here of what happened to me at your club: getting lost between the sauna and the cinema.'

Lately, I am told, there has been a brisk increase in proposals to remedy these rude amenities, and in some places the stuffed leather and wicker furnishings have been replaced by airport plastic. But no American wishing to help in the modernisation programme should dare to enquire the whereabouts of the 'Suggestion Box' unless he is ready to face the glowering eye of the Secretary and cower before the immortal line: '*I am the Suggestion Box!*' The Secretary, indeed, is a character quite unlike any official known to an American club. He is at once the manager, the senior starter, the rules administrator, the supervising treasurer, the *de facto* chairman of the board, and the Führer. His only counterpart in the United States was the late Clifford Roberts, the unchallenged dictator of Augusta National.

Finally, there is the game itself. There are middle-aged Englishmen, and Scots of all ages, who contend that foursomes (called but rarely played in America, Scotch foursomes) is 'the only game of golf and nae other'. Four players, as two teams, use two balls only, driving alternately and then playing alternate shots. The dwindling number of its advocates say that foursomes is the best team game, and the most rousingly competitive ever devised by a golfer. It does, of course, bypass any handicap system. And the British, aping Americans in their native competitive frenzy and their itch to flaunt an improbably low handicap, are succumbing in droves to the four-ball, five-hour match, and soon will be feeding their scores into the downtown computer that disgorges, once a month, a ream of handicap statistics on stock tickertape.

And, too, the British play golf everywhere on Sundays, a blasphemy long prohibited in Scotland. They have abandoned their old flannels and cricket shirts and, to the distress of the older members, the young now mimic the fine flower of the all-American dresser, even down – or up – to the baseball cap, or visor. They use fluffy or leather or polyester covers for their woods, where once they allowed them to clank and jangle in a canvas drainpipe bag slung over the left shoulder. They are losing caddies (to welfare) as rapidly as we are, and pull their clubs along in what they call trolleys and we call handcarts.

Electric carts are all but unknown. There are two at the oldest of British clubs, that of the Honourable Company of Edinburgh Golfers. But the vast majority of Britons have never seen one. The only one I ever saw in England was imported by the late Earl of Leicester from Germany, an armoured monster that looked as if it had been designed by a veteran of the Afrika Corps who had heard about a golf cart but had never seen one.

So the British, of all ages, still walk the course. On trips to Florida or the American desert, they still marvel, or shudder, at the fleets of electric carts going off in the morning like the first assault wave of the Battle of Alamein. It is unlikely, for some time, that a Briton will come across in his native land such a scorecard as Henry Longhurst rescued from a California club and cherished till the day he died. The last on its list of local rules printed the firm warning: 'A Player on Foot Has No Standing on the Course.'

27

No One Like Henry

1979

Everyone knows the special pleasure of discovering a new writer, even though the 'new' man may have been mouldering in his grave for centuries. The joy of discovering a new columnist is rarer. A columnist is of our own time and is not likely to have a point of view so far removed from the standard attitudes as to provide us, like, say, Sir Thomas Browne or Max Beerbohm, with an unexpected brand of common sense, quaintness or indignation.

But from time to time it happens. Some years ago, in San Francisco, I had just finished riffling through the two more or less compulsory New York magazines (the *New Yorker* and *New York*) and turned to the *San Francisco Chronicle* and came on a column by an unknown – unknown to me. His name was Charles McCabe. His piece was called 'The Good and the Chic'. He too, by some fluke of extrasensory perception, had in his hands the same two magazines. The *New Yorker* issue was eighteen months out of date but there were things in it that were permanently good. The *New York* issue was only two weeks old, but McCabe was already gripped by the fear that he was dangerously behind in knowing where to eat, what to read, what to think. The *New Yorker*, he concluded, was a good magazine; *New York* was chic, the epitome, he wrote, of 'boutique journalism'. Since then, McCabe is the first item I turn to whenever I am out there.

It is so with Longhurst. When I took up golf, lamentably late in life, I plunged into the golfing literature for instruction and into golf journalism for entertainment. I was not entertained. Most of the reporting I would later recognise as the best required much more technical knowledge than I then possessed. Herbert Warren Wind impressed me with his subtle and accurate knowledge, which plainly I must try to acquire; but in the meantime, I was a kindergarten arithmetic student stumbling around in a text on astrophysics. Pat Ward-Thomas, too, offered tantalising hints that in a year or two I might hope to appreciate why clover might require a hooded 5-iron or an innocent swale a lay-up. Of the others, Dan Jenkins was obviously having a lot of racy fun with locker-room know-how that was beyond me, and the American newspaper reporters seemed to be assembling and reassembling, week by week, a jigsaw puzzle of statistics.

But Longhurst wrote about the game as an entirely familiar exercise in human vanity. It is why, of all sports writers, he had for so many years the highest proportion of non-sporting readers. Izaak Walton on fishing, Dickens on lawyers, Mark Twain on steam-boating, Cardus on cricket: they have appealed for generations to people who know nothing about baiting a hook, filing a suit, taking a sounding or flighting a googly. Longhurst is of their breed. He is recognisable in the first few sentences as a sly, wry, rheumy-eyed observer of human beings who happened to choose golf to illustrate their fusses and follies. He might just as well have chosen oil-drilling, toboggan racing, military service, being a member of parliament or the motives that propelled an old lady over Niagara in a barrel. That, in fact, he wrote about all these things only went to prove his particular virtue: a curiosity that centred not on a game but zoomed in on whatever was bold, charming, idiotic or eccentric about human behaviour. After due meditation, he decided early on that as a weekly exercise of this curiosity, golf would do as well as anything.

In the beginning he served me, though he never knew it, as a canny uncle who was on my side against the commandments and prohibitions of my teachers. I was advised I must buy a 'matched' set of clubs. Longhurst said you'd do better with whatever you picked up that felt right. A tiger of a young pro in Los Angeles told me it was 'vital' to keep the right elbow practically knotted to the right waist. Longhurst said nothing was 'vital' except delivering the club head to the ball at a right angle. I was solemnly told to memorise the entire book of rules. Longhurst said you mustn't blow your nose when your partner was addressing the ball, but otherwise the book of rules was mostly nonsense.

Very many of his readers, I should guess, never got so far with the actual dogma of this or any other game. They were wooed and won by Longhurst's reminiscences of caddies who ranged 'from enchanting children to out-and-out brigands', by his affection for the praying mantis, by the boxing coach with 'traditional black cigar stub, unlit, who would have been ruled out of the average Hollywood film as a caricature', by the Dublin woman singing in the gutter and carrying a baby in her arms, 'possibly her own'. While his conscientious colleagues were calculating the yardage of the drives on the eighteenth of Augusta, Longhurst saw Weiskopf missing a tie by an inch and imagined him muttering, 'We was robbed.' It is the Hazlitt touch. Nobody remembers anything about the performance of the Italian jugglers who thrilled London in his day. But everybody remembers Hazlitt's remark that when anything at all is done so perfectly, you don't cheer, you cry.

From such an affable and sharp-eyed cynic, you must not expect starry-eyed tributes to the great ones of golf, or of any other game. Longhurst was as capable as any fan of a 'Hear, hear!' or 'Right on!' But there have been few sports writers so unfooled by the motives and the sought rewards of professional sportsmen. He could write with relish about cunning, skill, ingenuity, physical prowess, but he did not mistake games for the Battle of Britain or *The Pilgrim's Progress*. You must look elsewhere for rhapsodies about the courage, heroism, endurance or bravery of even the best of their time. I suspect he always knew that these words are better reserved for Scott at the Pole, Solzhenitsyn in prison or the long marches of Martin Luther

King Jr. As for the heroes of golf, he inclined to the scamps and the droll ones.

All these oddities, these agreeable and hilarious occasions, are written about in a prose style as effortless as falling out of bed: a more adroit achievement than some of his wordier rivals will ever appreciate. There are very few wasted words in Longhurst.

Enough. No tribute – to an artist, writer, musician, golfer or character, come to that – can equal the simple remark that 'there is no one like him'. Of course, each of us is unique. But the ability to put that uniqueness – however engaging or obnoxious – on to paper or over the box is totally beyond the multitude of people who would like to have a go at television or muse that one day they must 'write a book'. Let them bow before the fact that – there was no one like Henry.

28

Mark McCormack

2003

Who is Mark McCormack? The first time I was asked that question was nearly forty years ago, put by one of my oldest American friends. I was aghast, as one always is astonished at the ignorance of somebody on a TV game show who doesn't know something you know very well. (We accept – do we not? – without awe their knowing a dozen things we've never heard of.)

And then only this past week, when I said sadly over the phone, 'Mark McCormack is dead' – I received the same stony question.

To be candid, it is a good question. Just as difficult a question to answer as when you mention that Richard is a consultant, and the other comes back at you with: 'What is a consultant?' I was long frustrated at trying to find a sensible definition of the word till one day, years ago, I came on an old copy of the humorous magazine *Punch* and I was chuckling over a piece by a famous English humorist named A. P. Herbert. The piece ended with a sentence which I should have guessed could not have been written earlier than, say, the 1970s. But here, in the late Twenties, the piece ended: 'There will *always* be a consultant.' He was writing about a visit to what we used to call the doctor and is now called in this country 'your primary care physician'. He was remarking on the developing habit of a puzzled physician sending you to a specialist, known then (and since 1898, I find) as 'a consulting physician'.

Well, this hasn't helped me much with telling you what in fact made McCormack the world-wide pioneer of a profession he made his own. So this week I did a little more philological digging. And, more astonishing than anything, discovered that the first use of the word in English was in 1698. It is defined, in the 'Oxford', as meaning, then, 'A consultant – one who consults an oracle.' *That* doesn't help. McCormack *was* the oracle. He took on as clients people already famous in their profession, as golfer, opera singer, author, footballer, racing car driver, violinist, and – from time to time if they needed special help – a prime minister (Mrs Thatcher) or even a holy man (the Pope).

Let us begin with an approximate definition: McCormack was *the* creator of the talent industry: the making of people famous in their profession, famous to the rest of the world and making for them a fortune in the process.

Mark McCormack was born in Chicago in 1930, a fair, gentle boy with a feel for games. Unhappily, he was only six years old when he was struck by a car and broke his skull. He survived, under strict orders from the family doctor, never to play a contact sport. A taboo incidentally (or coincidentally) imposed on another great sports figure, Bobby Jones, as an ailing little boy. And so, as with Jones, the tender young McCormack was taken along with his father to the local club and taught to play golf. The small boy clearly loved the game and his father did the right thing, if he wanted his boy to become a golfer, as distinct from a man who 'plays golf'. He had him take lessons year in, year out from the age of eight. Consequently, he became a pretty good amateur golfer, doing something not achieved by one amateur in a hundred thousand: he qualified and played in the United States Open Championship, the United States Amateur and the British Amateur. But I don't believe he ever intended, for a second, to become a pro. He was a bright boy and took an honours degree in French at a famous Southern university – then a law degree (from Yale, no less) by the time he was twenty-four. After two years in the army, he joined a modest law firm in his native Midwestern city, Cleveland, at a modest salary.

He kept thinking he somehow ought to combine law with his favourite game. And in his late twenties, he had an idea. He noticed that even the best golfers earned no more than a fairly successful doctor or lawyer, but he liked the idea of helping great golfers to be thought of as movie stars, entertainers – and be rewarded accordingly. Where to begin, and how? It must have been a flash of revelation when he realised that the only top player he knew (and one who had just won the United States Open Championship) was an old college friend, a lean, athletic, attractive man in his late twenties, well known through television to thousands of fans. But how to make this young man wealthy beyond the hopes of avarice and leave a decent cut, perhaps enough to guarantee a living, for Mark H. McCormack?

By 1960, most of the leading players had somebody – a friend, a brother, a wife – make the travel arrangements for being on the tour, which starts in January in Hawaii, goes through California and the Southwest and the Deep South, then up and all over the country until the late fall. Mark McCormack said to Arnold Palmer: 'Let me take you over. I'll do all the arrangements for travel, and take care of hotels, all your bills, your taxes, the works. Furthermore, I'm going to get you to do TV advertisements for a whole range of things. Like? Like golf clubs, balls, clothing, whatever.'

'Whatever' came in time to be TV endorsement spots for an automobile, an investment firm, a bank, a watch, a department store chain, a brand of petrol, and an aircraft manufacturer. McCormack was to take 20 per cent of all relevant TV advertising earnings, 10 per cent of prize money on the tour, and 3 per cent of total salary. I have run into equally famous men who said they never would have said yes to those terms. And Palmer, earning 50,000 dollars a year in 1960 (about $500,000 today) must have thought twice. But if he did, on the third thought, he said yes. Four years later, his income had increased ten times. As Mr Micawber might have put it: 'Annual income ten million dollars, annual expenditure two million – plus 3 per cent to Mr McCormack. Result Happiness!'

From Arnold Palmer, McCormack went on to embrace Jack Nicklaus and other golfers. But why stop at golf? Came a time, say, thirty years ago, when stars of every breed and trade prayed and begged to be in the care of McCormack Inc. For by then he had set up his own firm, IMG – International Management Group. The main office is in Cleveland still, the other eighty-four offices dotted around nearly forty nations are staffed by around two thousand men and women. And by now, you don't have to wonder who manages the leading racing drivers, baseball and skating and basketball stars, opera singers, concert pianists – and how about Venus and Serena Williams? Of course. Itzhak Perlman, Pavarotti? Of course. Tiger? McCormack Inc. just signed Mr Woods to a new sports clothing deal for 100 million dollars over five years.

What is less believable at a first hearing is that he should have been solicited to help organise the ceremonies of such institutions as Wimbledon, the United States Olympic Committee, the United States Space Center, and the Nobel Prize Foundation. Oxford University once cried Help! And McCormack help was on the way.

The answer to the upcoming question is simple: McCormack was a great administrator, the General George Marshall of talent administrations. He gave the word 'management' a new magnitude. He planned every detail, anticipated every mishap. How would you care to organise, invent and arrange the physical tours of the Pope across friendly or hostile nations, to plan the details of, conveyance of, his protection (he had the bullet-proof, transparent shell invented)? How many police and plainclothesmen to watch an audience of a million listening to a pontiff whose medical needs called for special precautions as well as security? McCormack successfully took care of the scores of Papal journeys (as well as, I presume, of the Vatican portfolio).

As for the good fortune of the famous tenors, ball players, opera singers, sports stars that came under his protection? Well, to whom much is given, from them much is required. I remember a famous golfer – at drinks time – nervously looking at his gleaming, sponsor-donated, watch. He had to be up at dawn to go to Chicago and bless a manufacturing company's new line: his sweaters. 'And, oh my God, next Monday, I fly to Japan.' Playing there? 'No, no. I have to launch a chain of tea shops in my name.'

And maybe this weekend, you notice that the great Annika Sorenstam as she addresses the ball, is wearing on her cap the logo of the clubs she endorses; on her collar the logo of a food company; on the chest of her shirt – upper right a motor car logo – upper left a shirt maker; and, at the edge of a sleeve another reminder of her club manufacturer.

The gentle, handsome Mark McCormack worked steadily and ruthlessly every day from four in the morning on for his clients. I suspect he overworked, setting all these celebrities and institutions along their paths of glory. Which, as we all know, lead to only one place. And in his case, too soon. Last January, he had a massive heart attack and went into a coma – from which he never recovered. Last Friday, this remarkable man died, at seventy-two.

29

The Sporty Month

2001

I am looking warily through my study window, a sheet of glass too hot to touch, at an outside thermometer nestled cosily in a strip of shade. It says 101 degrees and looking beyond I see in Central Park great bulging forests of foliage seething in an atmosphere that the weather bureau gravely calls 'unacceptable' and the American Lung Association says is no fit place for joggers, respiratory patients or old folk. Early this morning, there was, panting round the reservoir, a single mad young jogger. He reminded me of my long-time doctor being asked, when the jogging mania came in, if he ever jogged. 'Only,' he said, 'when I'm late for the funeral of a patient who jogged.'

Now, I am unpacking the last dribble of personal belongings from the very small suitcase that I travel with, on the one or two times a year that I undertake a safari. After I'd rescued some newspaper clippings, toothbrush, pills, old boarding passes, I came on a little square card, one of a series that the San Francisco hotel puts on your pillow every night alongside a couple of mints. The cards are printed with single sentences written in tribute to the city by famous men. The one I'm look-ing at now makes me wish I'd never left the Golden Gate. It is that old chestnut of Mark Twain's, but generally unknown to outlanders. It says simply, 'The coldest winter I ever spent was summer in San Francisco.'

Of course, that ain't literally so, but it tells something permanent about the city that the city fathers would not like intending tourists to memorise. Namely, that July and August are the coldest months. And, all I can say, for people like me, who can no longer abide the midsummer sauna of this continent, San Francisco is, in those two months, a joy to be in. 'Cold' means daytime high temperature – 62, 3, 4. Over night-time – 52.

Alas, I am not there but here, where my morning newspaper has a half-page coloured map of the United States. Any place whose temperature is in the 50s is painted a pale lemon. Looking for that place is the old search for a needle. The wash goes yellow to orange, through scarlet to blood red (the 100s!). The whole country is scarlet, except the northernmost coast of rocky Maine, which is pink: in the 80s. But – but, on the very edge of the Pacific coast, there is a sliver, no more than an outline, of – lemon yellow. 'This is the place,' as Brigham Young said, settling the Mormons. Not in San Francisco, thank the Lord, though plural marriages have been known to exist in the city of St Francis, too.

This is August, what an old newspaperman called 'the sporty month' when the President of the United States sets the example by shelving the troubles and devoting a month to rest and play. Franklin Roosevelt used to go fishing. President Ford went high up in the Rockies, so he could see his drives off the tee actually go twenty-five yards beyond normal. President Teddy Roosevelt went shooting in the jungles of Brazil and fitted out one room in the White House with such a menagerie of heads and tusks that his successor had to take them down so as to be able to stand up straight.

It will not be amiss, I hope, at the beginning of this sporty month if I devote this letter to a delicious story, which (as Kissinger used to say) has the advantage of being true. It's meant chiefly for golfers and Scotsmen and Scotswomen though any other race, tribe, ethnic or sporting group is free to listen – at its peril. Since although the story is very simple, explaining the background for non-golfers might sound to some people like defining the opposing arguments in the Kyoto, or carbon-dioxide emission, debate, a subject I've spent a month trying to unravel. Unfortunately, my knowledge of higher mathematics, petroleum engineering and the economic potential of solar and other non-fossil fuels is so woefully inadequate as to disqualify me for an opinion. I must say I marvel at friends of mine, whose scientific bent does not bend over to the understanding of even a molecule who nevertheless have firm even indignant convictions about relative energy systems.

However, I feel on firm ground when the ground is one you trudge over in pursuit of a ball which, at one time, had a liquid centre. But then, one time, the clubhead of a driver was persimmon – now titanium.

Well, two weeks ago, on a Monday evening, an event happened in California unique in the history of the marvellous mania. The two best men golfers in the world teamed up with the two best women golfers to play a famous, weird desert course, where the fairways looked like irregular strips of green baize dropped in between a hundred piles of rocks, deposited (by dinosaurs, no doubt) on sand and scrub. Tiger Woods was partnered by Annika Sorenstam, the splendid perky little Swede. David Duval's partner was the Australian Karrie Webb, who a year ago – while Tiger Woods was winning five major tournaments out of eight to the howling applause of millions of new fans – was doing exactly the same to the stupefied admiration of the best golfers in the world.

The desert joust took place in the late afternoon merging into twilight and the purple desert darkness. Why? So that the sponsors of the tournament and the club, and, I guess, the chamber of commerce, could show off a new 600,000-watt system of high lights, which illuminated the thirty acres or so involved in laying out the fourteenth green and the last four holes. Is this the California – the 850 mile-long state that stands on the alert for instant blackouts because of its energy crisis? The same. Then why did they have to play this game at night? Nobody I've talked to has the remotest idea.

Well, the set up – a top man and top woman against two of their kind – was new. The format of the game was so new to Americans that the running commentator appeared to be talking to a four-year-old as he explained with kindly patience what he called 'this peculiar format'. Each team would play one ball. The man on each team would tee off, drive, on the odd holes – the first, third, fifth and so on; the women on the even-numbered holes. Thereafter, they would alternate strokes till the ball was in the hole. The game was to be match play – not accumulated number of strokes – but each hole a game in itself. If I already begin to sound peculiar, or slightly daffy to Scottish listeners, it's because this 'peculiar' format is what in Scotland is called Golf – or 'the gowf'.

It is astonishing but true that this 'peculiar format' is very rarely played in America. I have friends who have been playing with a golf ball for forty years and have never played it, and like my oldest friend, could not guess what it was like, as we started to play a famous links course at Brancaster, in Norfolk. As you approach the first tee, there is a big board planted firmly in a sandy hillock. It must have been there for decades. It says, 'No four-balls allowed on this course.' 'What,' cried my puzzled pal, 'what does it mean?' It meant exactly what it said. If you want to know what the American game of golf is like, nobody has given a more succinct, and I fear, scornful, description of it than the old rogue of golf writing, Henry Longhurst. After crying up the joys of match play, and the competitive tension and rare friendship that can be sustained between two partners with a single ball, he ends: 'To share a ball with a man or woman partner gives you a fellow feeling that no amount of four-balls, however successful, can ever match. This theory is fortified by looking at the opposite end of the scale, the four-ball at an average American country club, in which all four hole-out at every hole, their scores being carefully marked down (because they must know at the end "what they shot"), the whole indefinitely dreary business taking a minimum of four hours: it is one of the greatest wearinesses of the flesh ever voluntarily imposed upon man in the name of recreation.'

Well, the game we saw that infamous Monday night took four hours, even though it was the genuine article, imported from

Scotland in the long ago but since abandoned by ninety-nine Americans in a hundred. The game was long, slow and awkward-moving, and extremely humiliating to the four great ones, because of a totally unexpected novelty that will make this event for ever memorable. Each of the four champs played the worst game of golf any of them could remember. We saw that the incomparable Tiger can chili-dip a twenty-foot chip even as you and I; that Duval and Karrie Webb, also, can hit only two greens out of eighteen in regulation; that Tiger and Annika put each other into such preposterous lumps of scrub, cactus, mesquite and undergrowth that they each had to play left-handed.

The whole scene gave, need I say, great joy to every hacker on earth. My golf partner – my ex-partner (a surgeon who is also no slouch with a 2-iron, a 1-handicap from the championship tees at San Francisco's Olympic Club) – he gave me a parting word when I told him I thought I ought to talk about this dazzling event. 'Tell your people,' he said, 'that the Americans have finally discovered golf and found out it's a very difficult game.'

30

Codes of Conduct

1998

An American historian has just written a book about the decline
– perhaps the death – of a code of conduct that in some matters
– and in sport particularly – bound all of us together and was
taken for several generations, maybe for hundreds of years, to be
a guide to – or guarantee of – social stability. He might just as
well be tracing the history of the mediaeval tradition of chivalry
– an ethical ideal that started in France and Spain and spread
to England and was embodied in a code – a fusion, it has been
defined, of 'Christian and military conduct and still forms the
basis of the ethics of gentlemanly conduct'. (That was written
seventy years ago.)

Well, Prof. Digby Baltzell is charting the rise and fall of what's
left of the idea of a gentle man – in a sport! For two or three
centuries of an organised sport, the rules of those old mediaeval
ideals have been followed – though with a great deal less
flourishing of swords and halberds and no more proclaimed
devotion to the mistress of one's heart – who used to have to be
a virgin or the wife of another man – a standard of devotion that
at all times encouraged genteel monkey biz on the Lancelot–King
Arthur variation.

What has been bothering our historian since his retirement (he
is Professor emeritus of history and sociology at the University
of Pennsylvania) is the gross social jolt to his favourite sport of
tennis by what he calls 'the rise of the superbrat and the decline
in the idea of civility'.

Let me briefly sketch in the background of this grim period by reminding you that there are for professional tennis players about twenty-five, thirty tournaments a year, played in different countries – but there are only four major tournaments, which represent the national championship of each country. First, in January the Australian Open – next, in May, the French Open, end of June the British, known in Britain as, simply, 'The Championships' and, at the end of August, the United States Open.

This spring, on the last day – the Sunday – of the French championship, there was a rare and heartening scene. The two finalists were Spaniards, not surprising when you consider that they were playing on a clay surface (as are other Latino tournaments) and that the Spaniards are brought up on clay. After the last stroke was played and the winner ran to the net, his opponent ran with equal joy – they embraced, and the loser cried: 'Tonight, we celebrate together.' An old tennis watcher, who remembers other times, other manners, wheezed on a pipe and said: 'Reminds me of Super Brat and Old Nasty.'

New York City, August 1979, is a date that will live in infamy. John McEnroe, American, was to meet Ilie Nastase, Rumanian, in the second round of the US Open. I will not disgust you with the details, tho' if you'd been there, you might well have been terrified. To distil the awful occasion to its nasty essence – it was a breathtaking demonstration of superlative tennis, and granting that by that year the Rumanian and McEnroe were the leading exponents of tantrums and snatches of foul language tossed usually at linesmen and from time to time (just to show that they could stand up to any headmaster – as any juvenile delinquent should) they addressed a ripe obscenity at the chair umpire. In the fourth set, McEnroe served to Nastase who at once protested that he was not ready to receive. The umpire listened to Nastase's protest and a rising storm of clamour from the 10,000 spectators (it didn't help that the crowd decided Nastase was their boy). The umpire, applying the regular point penalty system, awarded the game to McEnroe. At which point, as Othello said, who was there, 'Chaos is come again.' Seventeen minutes of uproar and disruption – trash hurled on to the court, fighting broke out, police trotting – the umpire brought in the top man, the referee, who ordered Nastase to serve for the next game. Nastase said – in colourful words – No. Now, a rebellious player, according to the rules, can be given thirty seconds to repent and get on with it. The umpire waited just under a full minute and declared that Nastase had forfeited the game, set and match! That – in practically any other sport in the world – would have been the end of it. But now the crowd was seething – the tournament director an old champ himself – saw ahead a bang-up, bloody riot. He overrode the official decision, put a new man in the chair, and the match was played out, and McEnroe won.

Prof. Baltzell declared that scary night in August 1979 to mark 'the symbolic beginning of the roughneck age of tennis'. For the next ten years, Nastase found a worthy (if that's the word) successor in boorishness in one Jimmy Connors – and McEnroe grew in talent and brattishness to the despair of the tennis establishment and the pleasure of a new breed of tennis fan who came – to the US Open especially – looking more for mischief than great tennis, and accordingly got it. To allow that to happen over a whole decade was the sin of the tennis establishment, the people who ran the sport – both in America and in Britain.

Symbolically – as our American historian puts it – the end of the roughneck era came on the seventh day and the fourth round of the Australian Open in 1990. One Michael Pernfors – a low-ranking Swedish player (by the way, there has never, that I can recall, never been a boorish, a less than well-mannered Swedish player) – Michael Pernfors, then, was to play McEnroe who, in the previous rounds, had been at the top of his incomparable serve and volley – fine touch – form. But mark the glorious date: January 21st 1990 – midsummer in Australia. Five thirty in the afternoon – it's odd that the first act of this drama – considering that McEnroe's brattish behaviour had become by now a byword – it's odd that the first rebuke from an umpire should have been given to McEnroe for simply 'glaring' at a lineswoman. Then he was penalised a point for smashing his racquet on the court. Yet another typical McEnroe temper break – inaudible insults traded – referee brought in, told McEnroe to cool down and turned to leave. At which point, the one and only hurled a gutter obscenity at the referee and his mother. The referee turned back. 'No player,' he said, 'has ever spoken to me that way.' He walked off to the umpire. They talked together for a moment. The umpire nodded, rose to his chair and made a stunning announcement – which should have been made on many courts in many countries many times during the past ten years: 'Verbal abuse, audible obscenity – Mr McEnroe defaults – game, set and match to Pernfors.'

This outrage – so McEnroe and his millions of yobby fans thought it so – rang around the world. Fire McEnroe! Preposterous! Screaming bad language, stick-finger insults to the umpire – that was, by then, what half the crowd had come to see, wasn't it? Probably it was, and the retreat from bratdom was long and rumbling. But the Australians had struck a blow – you might poetically say for chivalry – and very soon a more positive cleansing act seemed to date the age of the superbrat once for all. The next year there arrived on the scene – as the new champion of the lists – a quite new character who loped around the court doing his business, which was to win tournaments, without grimacing – without charging the umpires – without complaint and with matchless talent. His name was Pete Sampras. And Prof. Baltzell, tho' still deeply pessimistic about the effect of money, money, money on manners (on and off the court), hopes the Nastase, Connors, McEnroe epoch is a part – a disreputable part – of history. Of the history of our society and not just of tennis.

In the wake of the United States Open (golf championship) and on the eve of the British Open (known to Britons simply as The Open) – I plainly can't help making an odious comparison with my own favourite game. I dared to make this point in sitting down in Florida, one warm night last March, when I had the honour of taking it up with some of the great old names, and minds of tennis. I was asked by a small, modest man who some people think is the best tennis player there has ever been – and himself a model throughout his career of impeccable conduct – why has there not been a nasty brat period, or even flashes of jerky behaviour – in professional golf – which has the same incitements of high nervous tension in situations promising equally preposterous amounts of money. I told him I didn't know.

For then, and for now, all I could say was that somehow – the etiquette of golf has been taught along with the rules – when promising players spend weeks at the professional qualifying school trying to get their playing card. Down three centuries the rules of etiquette have been as binding as those of chivalry – so much so that to this day watching a pro tournament, you can't tell who's the son of a truck driver and who's the son of a duke or a tycoon. The very idea of a player exploding over a marshal's or a referee's call is unthinkable. One thing I do know. If the old code has teeth and is applied strictly at all times and early enough – there will be no obscenities or screaming at officials and no riots.

I think of a golfer – a regular tournament pro – not absolutely top class but always in the running. Once he was seen stumbling over his ball and suddenly it quietly appeared not on the edge of the rough but on the edge of the putting green. He was severely warned. A few weeks later – the same thing happened again. Did he protest? He tried a mumble or two. Was he slapped on the wrist? Fined a thousand dollars? He was not. He was suspended, first, from pro golf – for life.

The last place in sport where an onlooker, a spectator, might get the impression that he is watching a modern form of the mediaeval joust – played quietly and strictly without tantrums by gentlemen is, I'm proud to say – the game of golf.

31

Prescription for a Pessimist

2001

This talk is going out, I just realise, on my daughter's birthday. I also realise, with a pang, that on this day she has exactly reversed the history of my exile. Having finished college, all pink and excited at the prospect of spending a year abroad, it now turns out she has been there ever since, having, like me, spent two thirds of her life away from her native soil. The ironic twist is that the place she chose to stay should have been England, so that she's exposed, among other hazards, to these talks and therefore is able to rebuke me, whenever she feels like it, on my subject matter. I have to say she's been mercifully sparing of such reproofs, but in view of the subject on which I was going to start this talk, I can never fail to remember her calling me up when she'd lived in London, only a year or two, suggesting that I make a point of talking about something other than – wait for it – golf! Now it's possible I may have taken up the subject twice in the previous six months. The trouble is she'd heard both talks. 'So,' she warned, 'go easy on golf. It is, after all, a minority sport.' Absolutely correct, except, that is, in Scotland and the United States, where two thirds of all regular golfers do not belong to a club but play on public courses.

Well the effect of that one gentle reproof down the years has been to terrify me into talking about golf not more than once a year, which was, always after attending as I did for thirty-five Aprils, the festival of the Masters Championship in Augusta, Georgia, on a majestic landscape which was less like a golf tournament than a royal garden party of the Hohenzollerns in a forest near Potsdam, perhaps. I go no more, mainly because taking two planes – one from New York to Atlanta, another one to Augusta and then doing the same thing back again – is to me an undertaking not unlike that of the one-legged man who decided to climb Mount Everest.

This overture, unlike most overtures, is not intended to give you a taste of the great themes to come, but rather to assure listeners (my daughter, for instance, if she happens to be on hand) that I am positively not going to talk about golf, even if the first little story I begin with suggests the opposite.

Very well then. We were sitting around at Augusta not so many years ago trying to agree on a list of the best half dozen golfers ever. Jack Nicklaus, then probably the best golfer who'd ever lived, said, in a relaxed philosophical moment: 'I don't suppose a day has gone by in the past thirty-odd years that I haven't at some moment thought about the golf swing.' The golf swing, even with the longest club, takes just on, or a fraction over, two seconds to perform. And it shows, among other things, what a world of nuance and subtlety lies waiting to be roused in those two seconds if the best player alive goes on, year after year, hoping to improve his two-second swing.

I can say with equal candour that since I arrived in Washington in 1937, throughout sixty-four years, I doubt a day has ever gone by when I haven't thought about government and governing, the art or business of turning political power into effective laws. That may sound a rather pedantic definition but I didn't toss it off casually. And neither Presidents nor lawmakers are to be judged by the way they flourish power, by their charm on television, their gift for words (Clinton talked a wonderful Presidency) nor even to be judged by the intelligence with which they grasp a great range of issues.

An old friend in San Francisco was recently reading over a list of Presidents, arranged in order of excellence or effectiveness, compiled by a posse of historians. And he asked me how my list would concur or vary. I had to say I have no list. It is impossible to set the achievements of any peacetime president or other democratic leader alongside the ones who presided over a nation at war. Lincoln, Churchill, Franklin Roosevelt, Truman, all had the enormous advantage of being able to suspend, for the time being, some of the essential protections of a democracy. Freedom of speech has to go, censorship has to come in. Lincoln, almost at once, abolished habeas corpus and threw thousands into jail without trial. Even considerations of humanity, which dare not be flouted in peacetime, have sometimes to be overwritten for the long-term good. When over three hundred thousand mainly British and French men were desperately being evacuated in every sort of boat and tub from the sands of Dunkirk, Churchill was the first to ponder the fact that all the allied materiel – tanks, guns, supplies, everything – had been abandoned. And that if ever British soldiers were to be rearmed and trained to re-invade France, they would have to be the fittest we could find. With this grim thought in mind (shared only with his doctor), Churchill ordered that the last people to be evacuated should be the wounded.

The American Civil War saw the introduction into a battlefield of the marvel of anaesthetics, administered by a dentist from Atlanta. For the first time in history an army could be spared the agonies of surgery – the Northern army that is. President Lincoln banned the shipment of anaesthetics to the Confederates.

Well the sentence that brought on this meditation was not meant to go into so serious a theme. I simply said that in sixty-four years there can scarcely have been a day in which I didn't think about government and its associated problems. I was going to go from there and say that during the past two weeks, I've been taking a holiday from political news and refreshing myself with daily viewing of the French Open Tennis Championships. At the end of it, I noticed that my view of people and the world has become more cheerful, more amiable. And from this has come a sharpening of a perception I had long ago which is, why certain friends I have, and certain acquaintances I used to run into regularly (or as Americans say, on a regular basis), are so upbeat, so light-hearted, so apparently untroubled in their view of life. For a short time before I had the revelation, I envied them, being myself naturally a short-term optimist but a long-term pessimist. Well, I discovered that the prescription for being so blithesome all the time is quite simple. It was one that all such people had followed most of their lives without, so to speak, knowing that they had a prescription at all. The thing to do is not to read a newspaper or watch the news. I was astounded when I heard from a close friend that he did neither. From there, down the years, in my infrequent but regular association with sportsmen, especially professional golfers and tennis players, I saw my original observation confirmed: golfers and tennis players (the pros I mean) spend all their waking hours playing their game or talking and arguing about it. The world of Washington, Africa, Tony Blair, the Balkans, AIDS, poverty, warfare, the United Nations, is a very faint sound, like a distant breeze, on the horizon. One of my favourite golfers was asked in an interview at the end of the last Presidential campaign how he felt about either candidate. This charming man, and most cunning, beautiful golfer, was dumbstruck in an amused sort of way. 'Candidates?' he said. 'How would I know? I don't vote. I'm not absolutely sure who's running. I'm not interested in politics.' He smiled, warmly shook the interviewer's hand, and turned back on the practice range and started stroking slow, beautiful 7-irons. I had admired this man, both his playing and his quiet amiable demeanour, for ten, fifteen years. I was staggered at his response in that brief interview. I still admire him. I also envy him, as I admired a whole clutch of new, upcoming players in Paris. Gifted, concentrated, and each day and all the days, utterly devoted to one thing in life: becoming better than they are – as tennis players.

32

Ghosts in the Mist

1995

Every great golf course has its heroes and its legends, which, however noteworthy, appeal exclusively to that tiny segment of society that is interested in golf. (According to a national statistical survey only 6.5 per cent of the American people have ever played, or watched, or read about golf.) But Shinnecock owns a legend quite apart from the world of golf, and the shocking truth that spawned the legend at one time engrossed the populations of New York and Pittsburgh, of London and Paris. The link between this society sex scandal and the comparatively chaste world of golf is Shinnecock's clubhouse planted up there on the hill directly off the through road. I think not of any golfer but of a ghostly threesome that still haunts the place: a middle-aged man about town with a bristling moustache and a blazing eye; a young, highly neurotic, Pittsburgh playboy, and the beautiful dumb girl who was the nemesis of both of them.

On pretty solid authority Shinnecock's clubhouse is down in the books as the first country clubhouse in America. Considering the high-toned social status that golf claimed here at the start – what with the Vanderbilts, and such, fetching golf clubs from Scotland in order to amuse themselves on their new playground on the South Shore of Long Island – we should not be surprised that they picked not a builder but an architect to design the novelty of a clubhouse, and that he should have been the most fashionable practitioner of his time. Stanford White was the man, an architect of astonishing versatility. Looking back over his work in New York alone, you could make a convincing case that no American of his time, and very likely no European, could design and reproduce to perfection all the famous orders of architecture.

The early bigwigs of Shinnecock Hills did not, of course, expect White to ornament their hillside with a miniature Taj Mahal. They were society burghers, and Stanford White was a social lion, able to accommodate all tastes. 'The best people', as they used to say, commissioned from him breathtaking grand churches, houses, memorials, and were not disappointed.

He had been a precocious teenage apprentice to H. H. Richardson, and when he was only twenty-six he polished up his professional escutcheon by joining the eminent firm of Mead and McKim. He was to become society's first choice to design a Gothic church, an Italian Renaissance mansion for the Velars, a Greek revival mansion grander than the White House for the Ogden Millets, a Gramercy Park clubhouse for actors, a Washington centennial, a Roman campus for New York University, a jewelled Byzantine cross for Eleanora Duse. He even designed a vast, exact copy of the Baths of Caracalla and called it Pennsylvania Station. (One of the more recent civic crimes was its destruction and replacement with a nondescript bus station masquerading as a railroad station.) The Shinnecock clubhouse was a comparatively modest effort with peculiar requirements (the Doges of Venice were not known to have demanded lockers and a golf shop) but White regarded it as one of several experiments he made to give substance and dignity to a native American form: the shingled country house. In the 1880s he had rented a characterless farmhouse on Long Island's North Shore, which he soon rebuilt and transformed into a three-gabled, arcaded, graceful country house, a style that served as a prototype for the clubhouse at Shinnecock Hills. It was, anyway, a relaxing change of pace from his most recent and dazzling project – a pleasure palace designed to replace the noxious abandoned train sheds used by Barnum for circuses and by evangelists for conversion. Only the name would remain the same: Madison Square Garden.

White's Garden comprised an amphitheatre to seat 10,000, a grand staircase, two restaurants, an assembly hall and theatre modelled after the Wagner Theatre in Bayreuth, and a roof-garden theatre restaurant. It was probably the most elegant of all White's buildings, a three-storey Italianate pavilion in white stone and terra cotta, colonnaded at the street level, surmounted by a more than 300-foot Moorish tower. White topped it off with a tower studio designed for his own occupancy, and for the occupancy of various transients, usually the pick of New York's – how shall we say – available young beauties.

When the new Garden opened in June 1890, White had been married for six years to a woman to whom he remained genuinely devoted for the remaining sixteen years of his life. A well-established domestic routine had him regularly taking his wife to Europe and joining her, in their Long Island retreat, on summer weekends. But he was free the rest of the time for his city devices. And while he may not, as the Pittsburgh playboy was later to testify, have 'ravished 378 girls', he did have lots of devices.

White called his Garden studio his 'snuggery'. It was the more conspicuous counterpart of another one he maintained on West 24th Street in a dingier part of town, a walk-up apartment, an unlikely location for a rich man's love nest but also a place he would be unlikely to be spied on.

Every first-time visitor surprised by the shabby exterior was immediately amazed by the opulence of the apartment at the top of the stairs: Italian antique furniture against scarlet flock walls, red velvet curtains that shut out the daylight, tapestries, paintings, everything glowing from invisible lights.

Beyond that a 'tiny mediation room', a cubicle of glass – walls, ceiling, floor – just managing to contain one large moss-green velvet couch. And up the last flight of stairs a splendid studio with busts, drawings, etched nudes and hanging from the ceiling a red velvet swing, for the preliminary exercises of Mr White's young ladies.

Into this delectable eyrie, one day in the summer of 1901,

came two young women. One was a voluptuous brunette, the other a sixteen-year-old Dresden doll. Both were in the chorus of the town's favourite musical, *Florodora*; the younger one defied every stereotype of a chorus girl. She was the baby of the show, one Evelyn Nesbit, an exquisite innocent with copper-coloured curls who had spent the past three years modelling for artists who recognised her on sight as the ideal representation of an angel (in a stained-glass window), as 'Dawn' or 'Innocence', as a water nymph, a shepherdess. When she first met White, she was also a virgin. (In the Hollywood version of the tale, produced – it ought to be said – forty years ago, she was played by Joan Collins.) Before the summer was over, Evelyn Nesbit was picked up alone at the theatre one night by White's regular cab driver and taken to West 24th Street. To put it crisply, she swung through the air on the red velvet swing. Stanford White broke out the champagne, and next morning Evelyn Nesbit woke up 'a woman'. Did Mr White, she wondered, suppose that the girls in the *Florodora* Sextette 'do these things'? Mr White, she later testified, 'sat down and laughed and laughed and laughed'. For the next two or three years, Evelyn Nesbit was White's favourite performer on and off the red velvet swing.

With tactful rapidity, we now dissolve not to a flash-back but to a flash-forward. It is eleven o'clock in the evening of June 25, 1906. It is the opening night of Madison Square Garden's summer musical, a rather listless piece called *Mamzelle Champagne*. The show is about to end with a fencing routine – the girls in tights – and a certain round of applause for the creator of this glittering roof garden, White himself, who is sitting alone at his regular table close by the stage.

Stanford White was now fifty-two years old, a handsome dark-haired, dark-eyed man, with furry eyebrows, a bristling moustache: a clubman's clubman well set up in the Edwardian manner, a man of boundless energy with a piercing gaze that had flashed many an early warning signal to many a guileless girl. He was nodding in his benevolent way to nearby friends and admirers and could not have noticed a much younger man sitting at a table for two on the far side of the room.

This rather unprepossessing thirty-five-year-old, a bespectacled bullfrog, was sitting with his wife of barely a year. Her name was Evelyn Nesbit Thaw. The man got up, threaded his way between the other diners and stopped at White's table. He put his hand in his breast pocket, took out a revolver and fired three times at the forehead of the astonished White, who fell dead on the instant. The young man walked slowly back to his table with his right arm high above his head, holding the revolver barrel down: a Florentine avenger signifying to the petrified audience that vengeance was his, he had repaid, and he would shoot no more. A fireman disarmed him, a policeman was sent for, and the man was taken off, unresisting, to the nearest station house.

It would be hard to imagine a more clear-cut case of premeditated murder. But several unmentioned factors combined to make the trial – the many trials – the most tortuous and avidly reported in American history, and the murderer's subsequent jousts with the law more interminable than any lawyer of the day could remember. (Of course, after the O.J. Simpson trial we now have a new standard by which to measure these things.)

To begin with, the man who shot Stanford White was no anonymous, off-the-street psychopath. He was a very rich psychopath. Harry Kendall Thaw was the heir to railroad and coke fortunes at a time when the earlier depredations of the robber barons had usually been expiated by a generation devoted to public service. William Thaw, the father, the majority stockholder in the Pennsylvania and other railroads, was famous not so much for his fortune as for the admirable ways in which he had spent it, endowing science fellowships at Harvard and Princeton and bestowing lavish gifts on art and education. The son, however, was a genetic throw-back to the lusty originals, and attendance at the University of Pittsburgh and at Harvard had done nothing to tame him. He was known to the newspapers, and the courts, for a whole routine of brassy escapades –

ending private parties with wrecked cafés, riding a horse up the steps of the Union League Club, staging vast and rowdy entertainments for scores of chorus girls, lighting cigars with the customary five-dollar bills.

Long before the shooting, he had become a public nuisance, and a nuisance spoiled rotten by a doting mother. She procured for him a fine defence counsel, including a florid San Francisco attorney famous for his passionate and effective way with juries. He bore the euphonious name of Delphin Delmas. From the start he chopped no logic, made no bones about the guilt of his client, but Delmas immediately scorned the indictment for murder in the first degree. Harry Thaw, he proclaimed to a startled courtroom, was sane both before and after the shooting but suffered in that one moment from a 'creditable' aberration, henceforth to be called, 'Dementia Americana'.

Thaw was, indeed, a new type of American hero, acting on an impulse, which in the wiser Latin countries had the full sanction of the law. He was simply asserting the unwritten law against a man who had betrayed his wife's honour. In short, Thaw was acting in the knowledge – which was true – that Stanford White had seduced Evelyn Nesbit before she was married, and had come to be horrified that his bride was – in the shameful language of the day – 'damaged goods'.

It is easy, almost automatic, for us to deride this turn-of-the-century rhetoric as so much period cant. But it did express a vengeful moral code of the time, which the victims believed in as solemnly as anybody. In fact, down the perspective of nearly ninety years, the main interest of the case to us is Evelyn Nesbit's almost evangelical view of herself as – what she testified in court – 'a ruined woman'. As such, she felt throughout two years of Thaw's beseechings that she could not possibly marry him, though she lived with him on a long European trip. When she finally gave in, Thaw began to beg her for repeated confessions of her association with Stanford White. Night after night, month after month, of their short marriage, she went through these ritual recitals, exploring – at Thaw's urging – more and more clinical details of her seduction. On the June night in 1906, he snapped.

The first trial ended with a hung jury. The second jury was bothered and bewildered by the expert testimony of five doctors, who found Thaw suffering from 'sub acute mania', or 'melancholia', or 'Romberg symptoms' or 'Argile-Robertson's disease' and/or several other afflictions long relegated to the psychiatric ash can. The second jury found him not guilty but insane, and he was committed to the state hospital for the criminally insane. It had been almost two years since White was shot, and most people assumed it was the end of the affair.

They reckoned without Thaw's mother, a woman of obsessive affection for her son and endless financial resources with which to search out hitherto undiscovered cracks in the iron body of the criminal code. She and her lawyers now secured a writ of habeas corpus. The demand for a third trial was met, throughout one year, by a series of dismissals, ending with one handed down by the United States Supreme Court. Throughout the next thirteen years, court reporters grew grey covering nothing but the legal campaigns of Harry K. Thaw: the bribing by Thaw of a lawyer, who was convicted and jailed; Thaw's escape from the hospital and his flight to Canada; his extradition and re-arrest and return to the asylum; the fleeting morale-booster of a music-hall song, 'Why Don't They Set Him Free?' ('Just because he's a millionaire, everybody's willing to treat him unfair.') On the uncontested evidence of his wife's several infidelities, Thaw eventually divorced her. And, finally in 1916, and at the end of yet another jury trial, he was declared sane and released to the bosom of his indomitable mother.

But even she, who had willingly testified in the later courts to her son's lifelong paranoia, had not guessed at the limits of his ingenious amusements. Only nine months out of custody, he was indicted for abducting and whipping a schoolboy, and adjudged insane once more and committed to an asylum in Pennsylvania. Seven years later, his mother 'settled' the abduction case out of court, and another sanity trial set him free.

On the 20th of May, 1924, he was, you might say, a free man, with no more obligations to the law after the payment of a $75,000 bill from the Pennsylvania State Hospital for superior 'board and lodging'. Throughout eighteen years, Mrs Thaw had proved, if proof were needed, that in the land sufficient tenacity and money can arrange to procure justice a little more equal than most. Thaw saw Evelyn on and off and, for some years, gave her driblets of money, which he frequently demanded to have repaid. He went off during the Depression on long safaris through the tourist capitals of Europe, and cut up in much of the old way, though staying on the safe side of the law. He wound up renting a house in Miami and died there, on February 21st, 1947, of a heart attack. He was seventy-six.

As for the lovely Evelyn Nesbit, for a few years she earned big money under the guidance of a flashy impresario, one Willie Hammerstein, who made the most of Thaw's escape into Canada by spreading gaudy stories that Evelyn went in fear of her life. He bullied New York City into providing her with a police escort, signed her to appear in his music hall and pocketed, at the end of a two-month run, an $80,000 profit. Evelyn made the European circuit, with a dancing partner (briefly her husband) demonstrating – as the poor man's Vernon Castle – the latest dances. As the years went by, first in cabarets and then in increasingly seedy theatres, she drew audiences bent on little more than fantasising her erotic history from the days of the red velvet swing on down to the fatal June night in Madison Square Garden. She made a few inconsequential movies. Her looks faded with the fading of her story. She ran night clubs here and there and saw them raided and closed as mobster properties. She became for a while a heroin addict. She went to Panama to perform in a ritzy bordello and was arrested for gambling. About the last that was heard of her was her employment, in 1955, on the movie *The Girl in the Red Velvet Swing*. For this depressing chore she carried, or endured, the title of 'technical adviser'. Finally, from a Hollywood rooming house, a reporter who had contrived what was surely her last interview, came away with the quote, 'Stanny was lucky; he died, I lived.' She died there, aged eighty-one, in 1966.

What was unknown to all but a few of the admirers and habitués of Stanford White's Madison Square Garden was the unsettling fact that even before the building appeared complete in all its elegance, the over-run costs were ruinous, and that through the next twenty-five years, it would lose money all the time. It must have been a great satisfaction to Harry Thaw in 1925, the year after he was set free, to watch the demolition of White's Garden by the wrecking ball. Its replacements, the Gardens we have known, have been – architecturally speaking – powerful contenders for the Warehouse of the Year Award.

But the Shinnecock Hills clubhouse still stands. A crusty old Long Islander, one of the original society golfers, maintained in his failing, and imaginative, old age that when the winter nor'easters whip across the Peconic Bay, the wind that soughs through the gorse and cedars is not the wind but the moans of the troubled spirit of Evelyn Nesbit. The rattling windows and creaking beams of the clubhouse are, of course, due to the post-mortem outbursts of Harry K. Thaw.

The Letters of Al Cooke

by Jerry Tarde
Chairman and Editor in Chief, Golf Digest

I sat down in the last row of the grandstand at Augusta National's 15th hole, and in one of those serendipitous moments, before I could notice the beige cashmere cardigan beside me, I heard that Voice – it was the host of *Masterpiece Theatre.** I mean to say, can you imagine a better way to spend a sunny afternoon in Georgia than watching the Masters first hand and listening to the commentary of Alistair Cooke in person?

It began a twenty-year friendship of letters and phone calls and the rare New York lunch. I fancied myself one of his golf gurus, a person he might call at odd times, at home, on weekends, asking urgent questions, like 'How many tournaments did Annika win last year?' or 'Why is Freddie not playing – I hope he's not trying to make a career out of television!'

I was always conning him to write for the magazine, sometimes successfully. I remember once pitching a piece about slow play, to which he responded:

April 23, 1989
I didn't forget your sly solicitation of me under the Big Tree. I will do you something, but I need a little time: namely to produce the hacker's definitive guide to golf. (I'll get a better, more seductive title.) Which entails bringing together the key bits of advice from Henry Leach to Ben Doyle. The point is that they all cancel out (e.g. Cotton – 'Hands are everything'; Nicklaus – 'The hands do nothing but hold on'). The

* A US television programme launched in 1971 and hosted by Alistair Cooke from 1971 to 1992.

earnest learner would be left with nothing but Percy Boomer's advice to 'develop feel'. Or, better, with the melancholy comment of my old Scottish teacher when I asked him if there was anything in – the then-raging fad of – 'Square to Square': 'Mistair Coooooke, nothing has evair been added to this game, since Braid and Vardon, aikscept an aikstra slice of baloney.' He talked more horse sense than any ten teachers I've ever run into. This might indeed serve as the text. I know it could be a funny and entertaining piece.

Patience. I have your number.

Best, Alistair

P.S. The chief trick of the piece would be not to point out contradictions but somehow to give the reader the exciting impression that one thing builds on another so as, in the end, to give him the perfect swing. Since Mark Twain is unavailable, I'll have to do my best.

To my eternal disappointment, I could never get the piece out of him, although other golf essays flowed such as 'Ghosts in the Mist' (Chapter 32), which ran in June 1995, the last time the Open was at Shinnecock. It is Alistair in his milieu – high-society sex scandal meets the murder of Shinnecock's clubhouse architect.

March 16, 1996
Alas! (a word I use only under the stress of great emotion) – I shall not be at Augusta this year. I'm going to the Lipton [tennis] next week, and three weeks after that back to San Francisco, where – two weeks ago – I sat for ten days waiting for the SFGC to dry out the course – for the first time in seventy years, they allowed no carts and closed the driving range . . . for eight days!!!! So I'm going to get in all those beautiful shots that were never played.

Regards, Alistair

Through the years, when he would call the office, the 'answering girl' (as he called her) would leave the pink slip in shorthand: 'Al Cooke called'. Whether she knew who Mr Cooke was, it's uncertain. But 'Al Cooke' is how he became known around the office. Of course, no one used it on him until one of our columnists wrote asking him to pen a testimonial for a new book jacket.

Oct. 7, 2002

This must be more brusque than it's meant to be. My constant companion, Arthur (Itis), restricts me to one letter a week. This is it.

I have never done solicited blurbs. Even so, I doubt I'd ever do one for a man who calls me Al! (In my ninety-four years, that's a first!)

Sorry. (I have to save my wretched hands for my weekly BBC Letter, now in its fifty-seventh year.)

Am I in good spirits? Yes. Am I healthy? You serious? I have not left this apartment since May, except when my wife/nurse takes me to the cardiologist.

Be well! Alistair

Phone calls and Christmas cards followed. And then the news that he was ending his *Letter from America* on the BBC after fifty-eight years and 2,869 letters. Two weeks later on March 30 he was gone. No more beautiful shots at San Francisco Golf Club. No calls in the night about Annika. No more trips to Augusta. *The Hacker's Definitive Guide to Golf* would not be written. Alas.

To paraphrase one of his own paraphrases upon the death of Duke Ellington, 'Alistair Cooke is dead. I don't have to believe it if I don't want to.'

Sources

Thanks are due to the following publishers and publications for permission to reproduce material:

'History of the Scottish Torture', originally published in the *New York Times*, 1973, and in *Fun & Games with Alistair Cooke*, Pavilion, London, and Arcade Publishing Inc., New York, 1994 (hereafter referred to as *F&G*)

'Fun and Games at Blackpool', originally published in *Blackpool Football*, Robert Hale, London, 1972, and in *F&G*

'Goodbye, Mr President, Hi There, Arnie!', originally published in *Golf*, March 1968

'Bobby Jones', originally published in *Memories of the Great and the Good*, Arcade Publishing Inc., New York, and Pavilion, London, 1999; 'The Gentleman from Georgia', originally appeared as 'What Have We Left for Bobby Jones?', the foreword to Martin Davis's *The Greatest of Them All: The Legend of Bobby Jones*, The American Golfer, Inc., Greenwich, Connecticut, 1996, and then appeared in a revised version for *Memories of the Great and the Good*

'The Missing Aristotle Papers on Golf', originally published in the *New York Herald Tribune*, Book Week, January 29, 1967, and in *F&G*

'Robert Tyre Jones, Jr, What Won the Grand Slam?', previously unpublished

'The Written Record', foreword to *The Golf Book*, edited by Michael Bartlett, Arbor House Publishing, New York, 1980, and in *F&G*

'Pottermanship', originally published in *Life* Magazine, 1968, and in *F&G*

'Walter Hagen 1892–1969', originally published in the United States Golf Association magazine, 1969, and in *F&G*

'Make Way for the Senior Golfer', originally published in *The Golfer's Bedside Book*, Batsford, London, 1971, and in *F&G*

'A Perfect Day for Golf', originally published in the *Guardian*, copyright © Guardian News and Media Ltd, 1968

'Snow, Cholera, Lions, and Other Distractions', originally published in *Golf*, 1975, a division of Time Inc., and in *F&G*

'Marching Orders', originally published in *F&G*

'Workers Arise! Shout "Fore!"', Letter from America No. 1350, first broadcast by BBC Radio 4, December 27, 1974, subsequently published in *The Americans*, Alfred A. Knopf, New York, 1979, and in *F&G*

'The Inauguration of President Grant', speech delivered at the annual meeting of the United States Golf Association, San Diego, January 1990, subsequently published in *F&G*

'Player's Puritan Victory', originally published in the *Guardian*, copyright © Guardian News and Media Ltd, 1965, and in *F&G*

'The Battle of Wentworth', originally published in the *New Yorker*, November 5, 1966. Reproduced courtesy of Condé Nast Publications

'Nicklaus: Twenty-two Years at Hard Labour', originally published in *The New York Times Magazine*, July 9, 1972, and in *F&G*

'The Heat On for Arnie & Co.', originally published in the *Guardian*, copyright © Guardian News and Media Ltd, 1968, and in *F&G*

'The American Tour Progress Report', broadcast by the BBC Radio 4 programme *Sport on 4*, May 20, 1978

'The Curtis Cup', originally published in the *Guardian*, copyright © Guardian News and Media Ltd, 1974

Letter to the Editor, *The New York Times*, previously unpublished

'The Masters: An American Festival', originally published in *Golf*, March 1975, a division of Time Inc., and in *F&G*

'Movers and Shakers of the Earth', originally published in *The World Atlas of Golf*, Mitchell Beazley, London, 1976, and in *F&G*

'Saying Farewell to a Departed Friend', originally published in the *Guardian*, copyright © Guardian News and Media Ltd, 1978, and later revised for *Golf Digest*, March 1983

'Golf: The American Conquest', originally published as 'Golf: The Olde-Fashioned Way', in *The New York Times Magazine*, March 31, 1985, and in *F&G*

'No One Like Henry', originally published in *The Best of Henry Longhurst*, Collins, London, 1979, and in *F&G*

'Mark McCormack', Letter from America No. 2831, originally broadcast by BBC Radio 4, May 23, 2003

'The Sporty Month', Letter from America No. 2738, originally broadcast by BBC Radio 4, August 10, 2001

'Codes of Conduct', Letter from America No. 2577, originally broadcast by BBC Radio 4, July 3, 1998

'Prescription for a Pessimist', Letter from America No. 2729, originally broadcast by BBC Radio 4, June 8, 2001

'Ghosts in the Mist', originally published in *Golf Digest*, June 1995

Index